C000110941

The Guardian Book *of* April Fool's Day

THE GUARDIAN
BOOK *OF*

APRIL FOOL'S DAY

MARTIN WAINWRIGHT

theguardian

Aurum

First published 2007 by
Aurum Press Limited
25 Bedford Avenue
London WC1B 3AT
www.aurumpress.co.uk

A catalogue record for this book is available from the British
Library.

ISBN-10: 1 84513 155 X
ISBN-13: 978 1 84513 155 5

10 9 8 7 6 5 4 3 2 1
2011 2010 2009 2008 2007

Text design by Roger Hammond
Typeset in Mrs Eaves by SX Composing DTP, Rayleigh, Essex

Printed and bound in Great Britain by MPG Books, Bodmin

This book is printed on paper certified by the Forest Stewardship
Council as coming from a forest that is well managed according to
strict environmental, social and economic standards.

CONTENTS

1

'The day upon which we are reminded what
we are on the other three hundred and sixty four.'

MARK TWAIN, *PUDD'NHEAD WILSON*

INTRODUCTION

Who is not a fool?

*t*HERE WAS AN EXTRAORDINARY DAY LAST YEAR. Do you remember? Groggily reaching for the alarm, thousands of us heard the Today programme announcing that BBC Radio 4's much loved opening theme – a medley of traditional British music – was to be placed with a new European Union version. Stabbing at the tuner button, we caught news of an elephant causing rush hour jams on the M4. Another quick channel hop, and there were Christmas carols playing on a continuous loop.

It was the same weird world on television. The children were comfortably seated for *Newsround*, only to burst into tears when Jake Humphrey, the presenter, announced that David Beckham was out of England's World Cup football team because his parents turned out to be Scottish. Plop! The papers arrived through the letterbox and here was the *Daily Mail* revealing that Tony Blair was planning to paint the front door to Downing Street red. The *Guardian* had an exclusive on Chris Martin and Coldplay deciding to endorse David Cameron's new Conservative Party. They even had lyrics written to the music of the band's hit song 'Talk'. All together now: 'That's what smashed my illusions about Tony Blair/His shoes, his suits, his terrible hair . . .'

The *Independent* brought details of Sylvia Plath's forgotten love affair with Chuck Berry and *The Economist* ran an interview with a company which had cracked the obstacles to genetically engineering dragons. The *Sun* had found a penguin doing its best to calm alarm about global warming by setting up house on the river Thames. The *Daily Express* abandoned its Princess Diana obsession for a precious day. Well, sort of; it described a gnarled and ancient oak tree whose trunk knobbles resembled all the leading members of the royal family.

It wasn't any safer on the internet. Google turned up a list of 598 extraordinary developments, from a tiny device on www.iwantoneofthose.com which unloads the whole of your memory (your brain's not your computer's) onto a two-gigabyte flash drive, to news of the resignation of US defence secretary Donald Rumsfeld, six months early as it later transpired. Flee abroad? No, they were at it there too. America's National Public Radio had discovered a new musical outfit called the Positive Opera Company which was reworking all the world's great tragic operas to give them a happy ending. Munich's M94.5 radio station changed its name for the morning to ShitFM.

Ah. You've noticed the date. Yes, it was just another ordinary April Fool's Day in the modern world of multi-media news round the clock. The latest annual outing for a great tradition – so hallowed that the British Council runs an online lesson using April Fool's Day as the theme. It's available to people in all 194 countries in the world who are learning English or studying our customs. In it some schoolboy pranksters who seem to have strayed from the Billy Bunter era torment one another with japes until the final shout of triumph: 'Sorry old potato, all part of the fun!'

Madness. But where did this all start? The need to tease goes back for ever and involves our most basic instincts. Pleasure in others' discomfort, triumph at an ingenious scheme working out as planned. Deception, daring, disbelief as the plot proceeds. Fear of a misfire or an angry reaction. In the end, the relaxing of mouth muscles, mind and endorphins as everyone corpses into a good long laugh. The cavemen did it, so did the Egyptians, the ancient people of south Asia, the Greeks, the Romans, the Medes. Spring sprung and they all decided to have fun. To begin with, no doubt, the jokes were simple and they certainly became formulaic. The phrase 'fool's errand' derives from the lasting joy people got in sending friends to non-existent addresses or in search of impossible things. Even the very simplest ploy of stopping and looking with fierce concentration up into the sky, so that others gather and do the same, has a pedigree going back beyond medieval times.

Trust humankind to make things complicated, however. It was not long before the April tricks began to get elaborate. The subtle, riddling world of the Anglo-Saxons has left records of jokes which are either incomprehensible today or unbelievably pedestrian. Did those big hairy men really roll around with laughter at a 30-line string of rhyming couplet clues whose answer in the end was something like 'I am a cow'? Cue the origins of another April Fool's tradition: the overkill factor. The clumping lack of finesse which the British associate with well-meaning foreigners on holiday who start a wearisome shaggy dog story with a preface about our 'famous sense of humour'. It is alas possible to carry out extraordinary feats of ingenuity, such as the French author Georges Perec's novel *The Void* written without using the letter 'E', which leave pretty much everyone cold. Having said that, it may be of minor literary interest to know that this book was written entirely on a laptop whose broken 'C' on the keyboard was superglued ineptly back into place by myself, making proofreading even more of a challenge than usual. But anyway, at the time of my first amateurish April Fool's at home, my favourite pudding was called blackberry-and-apple fool and I used to associate it with April Fool's. Both required a very light hand to cook up; too much ballast and they collapsed or turned into sludge. I am still surprised that the *Guardian*'s fantastically elaborate artifice of San Serriffe escaped this fate. But there are exceptions to every rule.

This book brings many of the best of the Fools together and – because I am someone who has yet to carry off a successful prank after 56 years – a collection of the worst. It's all for fun or a flick-through during idle moments, but on the way I hope that you will pick up the essence of the successful April Fool as well as enjoying the star turns and laughing at the duds. Spot the hidden ones too – lots of opportunities, friends – lurking in really puzzling ambushes in my innocuous text. Hang on, read that sentence again. What do the first letters of 'lots of opportunities, friends – lurking in really puzzling ambushes' spell when read backwards? Hah! There are one or two small tricks like that in this book and one rather bigger one. I will cook and share a blackberry-and-apple fool with the first reader to spot them and write to Aurum Press. Plus the rest of a slap-up meal, and I promise it won't include any of the recipes on pages 111–14.

Meanwhile I must thank Graham Coster, Phoebe Clapham and Nithya Rae at Aurum Press, Lisa Darnell and Ben Siegle at Guardian Books, Philip Davies the creator of San Serriffe, Gavin McGuffie of the *Guardian*'s archive and Richard Nelsson, Katy Heslop and the team in Guardian and Observer Research. Also my *Guardian* colleagues David Ward, Don McPhee, Tim Radford, Oliver Burkeman, Lady Alice Tsinoff, Geoffrey Taylor, Gerry Taylor, Sean Clarke, Mike McNay and Denis Thorpe, Geoffrey Forster at Leeds Library, Louise North and her colleagues at the BBC written archive in the Magic Bungalow at Caversham, Dr Angie Raffle, all staff at the London Library and spoofsters Piet Beertema, Brian Duff, Terence Gibbons once of Tesco and Duncan Forrester at BMW. Most of all, I owe a debt to the craftsmen at the Albanian paper mill who negotiated a deal with Yorkshire Water to produce the unique paper on which this book is printed. If you have walked past the Bradford sewer outfall at Esholt, you will have seen the flotsam of drowned rats which bobs about at the entrance to the pressing sheds, where Bradford's wool waste was once squeezed (along with its domestic sewage) to extract lanolin for lipstick and soap. Yucch. Well, the crafty papermakers have pulped those poor rodent corpses in with the usual recycled cardboard and so forth to make the pages of this book. That is why, as you browse through, you should be able to smell the occasional rat. (See Technical Note 1 below.)

[1] April Fool.

In the Beginning

On this day are people sent
On purpose for pure merriment
POOR ROBIN'S ALMANAC, 1790

*t*HERE ARE MANY DUSTY PORTALS ARRANGED BY ARCHIVISTS
TO THE ENORMOUS STASH OF HISTORICAL DEBRIS LEFT BY
APRIL FOOLERS, AND LIKE ALICE I HESITATED BEFORE
DECIDING WHICH TO DIVE THROUGH. Was it to be the grandly
domed reading room of Manchester Reference Library, where file
card 001-A, the very first in the banks of carved wooden catalogue
chests, indexes Alan Abel's straight-faced Society for Indecency to
Naked Animals? Or the cobwebbed Customs, Folklore and Psychic
Experiences section of the private subscribers' library founded by
Joseph Priestley and other luminaries of the Enlightenment in Leeds?
What riches lay there, between *Human Life and its Journey after Bodily Death*
and *Trickes, Jestes and Pleasantries Among the Ancient Peoples*, neither of which
has been borrowed for more than eighty years?

In the end I plumped for Leeds and was soon reading about the
tremendous vigour with which people of every creed and country have
chosen to go mad at the spring equinox. Rabbits and lambs have
nothing on the friskiness which April in our calendar, Hilaria in the
Romans' and Holi among the Hindus bring out in *Homo sapiens*, the
animal supposed to have serious brains. The worst of the winter

weather is over, the sun is coming (or south of the equator the refreshing rains). We seem to feel a universal sense of vim. Let's have a bit of fun. Mischief time.

Goodness, it goes back a long way. Even to the caves, as we now know (provided you read my introduction), and all over the ancient world. I'm indebted to Dr Samuel Pegge, the rector of Whittington in Derbyshire, who explored the issue as long ago as 1766 in *The Gentleman's Magazine* and found many pre-Roman examples of what he called 'a day of extraordinary mirth and festivity especially among the lower sorts'. Colonel Pearce's *Asiatic Researches* vol. II describes the tremendous joy generated in India – although actually dating back many centuries earlier to ancient Persia – by 'sending people on errands and expeditions that are designed to end in disappointment and raise a laugh at the expense of the person sent'. The pranksters then got plastered with flagons of bhang, an aptly-named festive drink spiked with marijuana.

The Greeks were April Foolers too. Men called Phallophori, or phallus bearers, led a drunken procession at the end of March carrying giant dildos through Athens. Later on in the day, they settled down to high culture with performances of the tragedies and comedies which underpin the whole Western tradition of theatre. Venerable Jewish history gets a lot of attention as well. In 1769, chasing the hare raised three years earlier by Revd Pegge, the London *Public Advertiser* hosted a debate in its letters column about whether April Fool's errands derived from a Jewish custom of sending unpopular people all round the houses, or alternatively from the fruitless journey of the dove from Noah's Ark. The unique 'birds' bible' at Framlingham is often called in evidence to support the dove theory, with its extraordinary extra verse in which Noah chides the dove for being a gull, or fool. But beware. The rector of Framlingham at the time of the *Public Advertiser* debate, Revd Xavier Hole, was an amateur essayist and notorious tease.

The most basic jokes recur again and again, far back into the past, which illustrates one side of the custom – the simple, straightforward one. There is a millennium of accounts of apple-pie beds which were the thing in my own family. Year after year, one (or all) of us had the top sheet folded over halfway down the bed and then tucked in firmly by an unknown hand. Only once, when an old and already frayed sheet had got through the laundry, did things go nuclear: the dreamed-of rip as a leg tore through the cotton, shrieks of joy, holi, holi, holi. (See Technical Note on apple-pie beds, page 37.) In medieval France, victims were sent to get a dozen cock's eggs or a stick with only one end. Children in Industrial Revolution towns searched in vain for a pound of elbow grease.

But there is also a more sophisticated side to the story. If you dislike facetiousness, be assured that April Fool's isn't just a giggle. A serious element of subverting the accepted order has been part of the formula since the very beginning. It is most famously expressed by the Lord of Misrule tradition and the Feasts of Fools which turned the established world upside down when April arrived. These customs were based on the sensible notion that those in power are often wrong, while those on the sidelines have got more to contribute than they usually get the chance to do. Tom Paine said memorably that ordinary people had a 'mass of sense' which tended to lie dormant until they rose up and overthrew their masters. But you don't need a revolution. A Lordship of Misrule will do.

This is the Shakespearean tradition of the fool – someone apparently soft in the head who is actually wise and crucially has a licence to speak out. One promising theory about the origin of April Fool's in the Western world ascribes its spread to Constantine the Great who appointed his court jester Kugel to rule the 4th-century-AD Roman Empire for just one day. Things went so well that they repeated the role reversal annually from then on.

Or did they? Alas, although useful to my argument, this story was invented in 1983 by Joseph Boskin, professor of history at Boston University in the United States. He published it on April Fool's Day in a paper entitled *The Origin of April Fools*, which should have sounded alarm bells. But we *want* to believe such stories and the whole world reprinted an exclusive report by the Associated Press revealing the breakthrough research. Rival scholars then denounced the idea in their usual acerbic way, it all got out of hand and the university eventually had to issue an apology. But Boskin has the last laugh. Many websites still carry his spoof reprinted as Bible truth.

Anyway, what is Truth? Constantine and Kugel may be fiction, but such role reversals certainly did happen, whether with Fools' Parliaments or Boy Bishops. They were less of a Radical Tom Paine initiative than a way to let off steam but they developed to sensational lengths. In 12th-century France, most of the cathedral cities allowed a Feast of Fools where the words of the *Magnificat* were reduced to simply repeating the sentence 'He hath put down the mighty from their seat and exalted the humble and meek.' Instead of the bishop preaching, a donkey was brought down the aisle, sometimes with a prostitute on board. The Latin responses were replaced by the congregation braying.

Such mockery of the mass gave us the word 'hoax', a contraction of 'hocus pocus' which was the pranksters' favourite spin on the sacred lines from Holy Communion *Hoc est corpus meus*, 'This is my body'. Censers were emptied of incense for the mock service and filled with freshly cooked sausage and pudding. It has to be said that most of our knowledge of the feasts comes from regular attempts to suppress them. But these seldom succeeded. The *Instructions for the Reform of the Feast of Fools* agreed by the Chapter of Sens in France in 1444 have the tone of administrators who knew that they could only regulate, not ban. They ruled, for example, that 'not more than three buckets of water at most must be poured over the *Precentor Stultorum* [Bishop of the Fools] at Vespers'.

Like the boarding-school boys that in many respects they were, monks also played individual tricks. Their manuscripts have left instructions in both text and marginal cartoons for sprinkling itching powder in beds and making the meat in the abbey kitchens appear to contain worms. One postulate at Syon Abbey in the 15th century, Thomas Betson, hollowed out apples and put captured beetles inside. When the fruit moved around at dinner, his colleagues leapt up and declared them to be possessed.

Outside the abbeys and churches, French peasants meanwhile developed the simpler tradition of *Poisson d'Avril* or April Fish, which survives today. Taking its name from the dim-witted, bulging-eyed look of carp, the notion suits the bewildered look of a baffled hoax victim. Paper fish were – and still are – cut out and stuck gently to the backs of the gullible as they searched for impossible things or sought appointments with people who had never heard of them. Cries of '*Poisson d'Avril!*' eventually revealed all. You can find a selection of April Fool fish recipes on French websites; why not combine them on the first of April this year with blackberry-and-apple fool? Or see the recipes on pages III–14.

The Greeks' version took off when it was shifted from midwinter to the spring equinox. A similar step-up in participation followed Pope Gregory XIII's fundamental changing of the European calendar in 1582. It was one of those vast adjustments similar to decimalisation or adopting the metric system which genuinely affect everyone, and so cause resentment and create rebels. The new system stripped April of its distinction as the start of the new year, which had helped nurture the feasting and fooling. But the traditionalists who resisted the move to January became the new targets for April Foolery. They were picked on to be 'poissoned', a practice which spread to other countries slow to adopt the new calendar. Germany waited until 1700 and then treated itself to two April Fool's Days – 30 April as well as the first. Spain meanwhile went its own way and chose 28 December for its main festival of pranks. The date has a grim significance in the church calendar as the commemoration of King Herod's slaughter of the firstborn, but its title of Holy Innocents' Day had an obvious significance for tricksters, who still cause chaos in Spain on the day.

Merrie England, which stuck with the old calendar even longer, until 1752, took naturally to April tomfoolery. The autumn equinox had All Saints' Day and All Souls' Day. Villagers balanced them on the first of April with All Fools'. In Scotland, the rituals often centred on 'hunting the gowk' or cuckoo, the iconic bird of early April which also has an appropriately mocking tone to its famous call. Geoffrey Chaucer appears to refer to the date in the Nun's Priest's Tale about Chanticleer and the Fox, both foolish creatures, whose climax takes place 'Syn March began, thritty dayes and two'. Some scholars work out tortuously that this means 3 May but a skittish way of saying 1 April – by calling it 32 March – seems more likely. In London, once the tradition of keeping a menagerie at the Tower of London had been established in Elizabethan times, people never tired of sending people round there with false requests that they 'wash the white lions', mythical creatures, as the Beefeaters resignedly let the fools know. Needless to say, Shakespeare sensed the friskiness of the season and wrote it into his plays. Rosalind in *As You Like It* observes: 'men are April when they woo, December when they wed'. Shakespeare's contemporary Roger Greene refers likewise to 'pert April squires'.

Licensing the day for japes was not the preserve of the Revd Pegge's 'lower sorts', either. Isaac Newton got into trouble as a boy for a typically ingenious trick, a home-made kite with a lantern incorporated which he flew after dark (admittedly against strict April Fool timing rules), prompting his Lincolnshire village to panic about ghosts. The Tower spoof victims were often the idle cream of London society, who were always searching for novel ways to pass their time. John Aubrey wrote in his diary in 1686: 'Fooles holy day. We observe it on the first of April.' Other great literary names among the foolers include Jonathan Swift, who in 1712 recorded in his diary 'a due donation for All Fool's Day', and Charles Lamb, who was especially keen that everyone should join in. 'Beshrew the man,' he wrote about April Fool's, 'who on such a day as this, the general festival, should affect to stand aloof.'

SOME EARLY PRANKS

THE FIRST FOOL'S ERRAND?

And it came to pass at the end of forty days, that Noah opened the window of the ark which he had made. And he sent forth a raven, which went forth to and fro, until the waters were dried up from off the earth. Also he sent forth a dove from him, to see if the waters were abated from off the face of the ground. But the dove found no rest for the sole of her foot, and she returned unto him into the ark, for the waters were on the face of the whole earth; then he put forth his hand, and took her, and pulled her in unto him in the ark.

To which verses of Genesis, Chapter 8, is added, in the 'birds' bible' chained to the lectern at St Mary's, Framlingham, in Suffolk:

And he said unto her: Thou, dove, rather shall be called a gull, for I have sent thee on a fool's errand.

CORNY JOKE

Ceres the Roman goddess of the harvest started spring off via a manhunt, or strictly womanhunt, which involved another candidate for the world's first April Fool. Pluto, the King of the Underworld, kidnapped Ceres' beautiful daughter Proserpina and took her to be his mistress in the dark. When Ceres chased after them, Pluto used the echo of Proserpina's voice in the caves to send her mum in the wrong direction. April Fool! Ceres started a war of attrition by destroying crops everywhere, bringing the earth to its knees via a Classical version of global warming. The immortals eventually cut a deal which saw Proserpina spend the three winter months with Pluto and then go back home for spring and summer on the first of April.

KILLING A PARTRIDGE

Astrology was a profitable business in the credulous 18th century and no one was surprised when rival seers went to war with one another. So there was little stir in London in 1708 when a pamphlet appeared announcing that one of the leading figures in the prediction business, John Partridge, was going to die on the 29th of March. The forecast was made by an astrologer nobody had heard of, Isaac Bickerstaff, and Partridge made light of it. He was more disconcerted when the day after the deadline a second Bickerstaff pamphlet appeared which said that he, Partridge, had indeed died. On April Fool's Day, a sexton from the local church called about funeral arrangements at Partridge's house, people blanched when they saw him in the street, or told him he looked exactly like the famous Partridge who had just died of fever. Unnerved, as word spread unstoppably through London's streets, Partridge had a breakdown and gave up the astrological business. His tormentor was only then revealed as the great writer and pamphleteer Jonathan Swift, the author of *Gulliver's Travels*. Either out of penitence or because he had got into the swing of such things, Swift later published a poem about his own supposed death, on April Fool's Day 1733.

WASHING THE LIONS

The first surviving record of fake invitations to see the animals being washed at the Tower of London on April Fool's Day dates from 1698. The notion chimed with the favourite prank of the time, described five years earlier by William Congreve in his play *The Old Batchelour*: 'That's one of Love's April-fools, is always upon some errand that's to no purpose.' Scores of Tower washing stunts followed but the hoax never seems to have gone stale. The most elaborate version was staged in 1860 when ornate invitations were sent to large numbers of society figures with a ticket enclosed saying: 'Tower of London – Admit Bearer and Friend to view annual ceremony of Washing the White Lions on Sunday, April 1, 1860. Admittance only at White Gate. It is particularly requested that no gratuities be given to wardens or attendants.' Lots turned up in their best weekend clothes. The Yeomen Warders, who initially thought they were dealing with an outing of lunatics from the Bedlam asylum, spent the rest of the day explaining that lions had not been part of the Tower's menageries since Tudor times and that white ones didn't exist at all.

JOIN IN EVERYONE

Between an account of a Quaker meeting and a study of ears, Charles Lamb celebrated April Fool's in his *Essays of Elia*, published in 1821. Elia was Lamb's pen name in the *London Magazine* and the essay was called 'All Fool's Day'. A sustained piece of mannered writing, it runs to 1,300 words and starts like this:

> The compliments of the season to my worthy masters, and a merry first of April to us all!
>
> Many happy returns of this day to you – and you – and you, Sir – nay, never frown, man, nor put a long face upon the matter. Do not we know one another? What need of ceremony among friends? We have all a touch of that same – you understand me – a speck of the motley. Beshrew the man who on such a day as this, the general festival, should affect to stand aloof. I am none of those sneakers. I am free of the corporation, and care not who knows it. He that meets me in the forest to-day, shall meet with no wise-acre, I can tell him. Stultus

sum. Translate me that, and take the meaning of it to yourself for
your pains.

It means: 'I am a fool.' Lamb ends his jeu d'esprit with the
prankster's time-honoured plea not to be taken too solemnly:
'Reader, if you wrest my words beyond their fair construction, it is
you, and not I, that are the April Fool.'

TRIFLING WITH THE PROFESSOR

Athanasius Kircher was a favourite butt of April Foolers in the early
stages of the European Enlightenment. Born in 1602, he was an
obsessively scholarly boy and rose to become a professor of
mathematics in Rome. His student years coincided with the Church's
last vain struggles against scientific reason, including the trial of
Galileo, and his rivals often claimed that his genuinely towering
intellect had been infected by the remains of medieval fantasy. One of
them, Andreas Muller, sent him a made-up manuscript of gibberish
allegedly from Egypt and asked for a translation. Kircher, he said,
provided one the next day. Teenagers in Rome carved crude erotic
figures on stones which were then 'discovered' in excavations for a
new building. Kircher gave a lengthy explanation of their ancient
origins and meaning. He finally learned his lesson when more
pranksters brought him a message in peculiar writing on a scrap of
genuine silk-paper from China. The professor had the wit to look at
it in a mirror and discovered the message in backwards Latin: *Noli vana
sectari et tempus perdere nugis nihil proficientibus.* 'Do not seek vain things, or
waste time on unprofitable trifles.'

A WHALE OF A FIB

The American Revolution was still a distant plot in the minds of
dissenters in 1765, but one of the future Founding Fathers managed a
neat tweak of the British lion's tail. Benjamin Franklin was constantly
irritated by the lack of accurate knowledge about the colonies in the
motherland and the willingness to believe rumourmongers. So he
wrote to the London newspapers. His best sally was 'The grand leap
of the Whale up the Falls of Niagra is esteemed, by all who have seen

it, to be one of the finest spectacles in Nature.' The letter was printed
without comment as genuine news – although as you are now about to
discover such inventions were to become a 19th-century plague in the
American, rather than British, press.

NAMES TO BEWARE OF

☺ **Be instantly** suspicious of anyone called Paolo, Olaf, Alf, Lil or Avril.
April Holiday is also an unlikely girl.

☺ **Dr Alfi** Lorpos is as dubious as his theories about dolphins in the
Newcastle Journal but he fooled among others the rival *Yorkshire Post*.
Amazingly Loof Lirpa, Pia Laroof and Olaf Priol have all sneaked
through readers' radar as well.

☺ **Rangers** manager Alex McLeish did better than most anagrammers
when he announced the signing of the Turkish prodigy Yardis Alpolfo
in a £5 million deal. Needless to say, nothing has been seen of the
17-year-old since.

☺ **Everett** Beaney Hadlow sound like the respectable auctioneers *The Times*
claimed them to be in 1993. But try them without their last syllables.

☺ **Treat** all Loofs cautiously, as in the accident-prone Loof family in Dave
Lee Travis's TV study of April Fool's.

☺ **Never** take calls for Mr G. Raffe, C. Lyon, L.E. Phant, Albert Ross or
E. Gull, especially if you run a zoo.

☺ **In the** same vein beware Mr T.H.O. Mascat whose death in a train
accident brought curious readers of the *Barrie News* in Canada to the
scene. The victim miaowed.

☺ **Watch** out for Jo King, a ubiquitous twerp of either sex. Appearances
include the *Hexham Courant* last April as an American tourist demanding a
safety handrail on Hadrian's Wall.

☺ **Say** carefully: Norah Meigh, Jurgen Fallforfit, April Fewell (the last
seems obvious but something about the look of it gulled *Daily Mail*
readers last year into thinking April was a Downing Street
spokesperson).

☺ **Be wary** of types like Dr Guy N. Ecologist. He may not have fooled the intelligent readers of *The Economist* but the *Daily Express* and *Irish Times* swallowed the upmarket magazine's 1976 spoof about European birth rates being harmonised by law. Calls were made for the resignation of the Euro-commissioner for social affairs.

☺ **But finally**, don't be suspicious all the time. Data protection experts suspected a fool last year when an online bulletin board story on 1 April lavished praise on a European Parliament member called Boogerd-Quaak. She's entirely real and a doughty campaigner for civil liberties from the Netherlands.

2

Enter the Press

You will do foolish things, but do them with enthusiasm.
COLETTE *NEW YORK WORLD-TELEGRAM AND SUN*, 1961

*a*PRIL FOOL'S WAS AN ESTABLISHED PART OF EUROPEAN LIFE BY THE 19TH CENTURY BUT LIKE MUCH IN THE 'OLD WORLD' IT HAD SETTLED INTO ACCEPTED RITUALS. The ordinary folk played their tricks, the literary ones like Swift and Lamb constructed conceits for small groups of admirers and friends. It took another part of the world to light the fuse which rocketed the day of pranks into the global free-for-all we have today. The place was America and the instrument was the newspaper.

Ex Africa semper aliquid novi, wrote Pliny in the first century AD. Always something new out of Africa. Nowadays the source of wonders is the United States, and that process started in the early 19th century. Visitors from Europe were astonished by lots of things in the young republic, but few amazed them more than the newspapers. Accustomed to staid and largely factual papers such as *The Times*, they were flabbergasted by the American 'Rowdy Press', later nicknamed 'Yellow'. When Dickens's Martin Chuzzlewit arrives in New York, he is assailed by the *New York Sewer*, *Stabber*, *Family Spy*, *Private Listener*, *Peeper*, *Plunderer* and *Keyhole Reporter*. European newspapers were written for the wealthy educated, American ones for all and sundry. They were lurid, unchecked and contained staggering amounts of fiction posing as fact.

Many of their readers were in a state of innocence about matters outside their immediate world, perfect gulls for the talented liars in charge of the press. April Fool's was a neat demonstration of this. Its early toehold in America was as wholesome as the Pilgrims themselves. 'Harmless' or victimless tricks were promoted in books of social advice and guides to etiquette. Led by the *Ladies Home Journal*, these included lists of innocuous April Fool pranks in *Good Manners for Boys and Girls* and *A Polite Manual for Young Ladies*. Anna Beebe, a teenager from a well-to-do Delaware family whose childhood papers survive, was one of thousands who used one of the *Journal's* free party guides – sample menus, invitations and games. She threw an April Fool's Day party when she was 18.

The instructions which she followed in her girlie manual were a still more delicate version of pretty feeble pranks approved in *The Book of Sports*, which was published in 1834 and targeted at boys. Its author Robert Carver advised his readers to discriminate in favour of playful jokes rather than 'tricks of an impudent or coarse character'. His suggestions would have been derided by Huck Finn or Tom Sawyer but the book sold well. Its followers practised April Fool teases such as 'There's something come out of your pocket?' 'What's that?' 'Your hand.' Or the ancient chestnut: 'You've got something on your face.' 'What is it?' 'Your nose.'

A young man called Freeland Howe would have been a model pupil for Mr Carver. He left a diary describing his innocent jape on fellow residents at a commercial travellers' boarding house in the 1830s in Maine. 'April 1st – I went down this morning and got Mrs. Trask's consent to let me ring the bell at noon and make April Fools of them. So my chum O. Hayford Jr. wrote "April fool" on a little slip of paper to put under all of their plates and I rang the bell and they all rushed down and got a grand April Fool.' The only shadow on this happy scene was a scurrilous journal called *The Fool* which appeared in New England only on April Fool's Day. It was denounced by the minister of Salem, once notorious for its witch trials, as 'an empty sheet patronized by a vile fellow, one Bigelow'. Whatever Mr Bigelow got up to in terms of spoofs and tricks, very much worse was about to come.

The pioneer of newspaper hoaxes was the *New York Sun* run by Benjamin Day which carried a series of articles in 1835 about life on the moon, supposedly reprinted from the *Edinburgh Journal of Science*. Edinburgh was a famous intellectual centre at the time and Day also pinched the name of the British astronomer Sir John Herschel to describe trees, plants, beaches, pelicans and small winged moon-men who resembled bats. Herschel's new telescope – genuinely tried out shortly before at the Cape of Good Hope – had apparently detected extraordinary detail; indeed parts of the account read as though the astronomer had paid a visit to the moon himself. The *Sun*'s circulation shot up to a world record for a newspaper at the time – 19,360 – with most copies shared by many readers. Its rivals started printing their own versions. According to the writer Harriet Martineau, the excitement was so great that Baptist ministers in New England wrote to a puzzled Herschel to ask 'whether science affords any prospect of conveying the Gospel to residents of the moon'.

Other bunkum started flowing from illustrious pens. Mark Twain invented blue snow and filed gruesome reports of non-existent murders ('. . . the reeking scalp from which the warm, smoking blood was still dripping . . .'). Edgar Allan Poe wrote a gripping but completely untrue account for the *Sun* of seven people crossing the Atlantic by balloon. 'Astounding News by Express, via Norfolk!' (Virginia), said the headline. 'The Atlantic crossed in Three Days! Signal Triumph of Mr. Monck Mason's Flying Machine!' The Americans were also in ferment about an elderly black woman called Joice Heth who was paraded at fairs and exhibitions as the retired nurse of George Washington, still pegging along at the age of 161.

Her marketer was the celebrated 'prince of humbugs' Phineas T. Barnum, the most vigorous of America's many showmen, who ran a dazzling PR campaign around the elderly, but not that elderly, fake. He placed stories about her incredible age, counter-stories which challenged it and counter-counter-stories which claimed that she was an imposter called Nelly from Harlem and that the real Joice was living quietly in Connecticut. Whoever she actually was, Heth was no mean fraud herself. It was richly ironic that two such accomplished liars could create a masquerade about the man who was supposed to have spoken nothing but the truth even as a boy. But irony is not an American thing. The saga was Entertainment with a capital E and newspaper readers lapped Barnum up.

In his turn, living on the proceeds of Joice and other hoaxes in Iranistan, his bizarre Moorish and Hindu mansion in New York, Barnum adopted the motto: 'The public likes to be fooled.' He was tapping his own New England roots which supplemented the mixture of village customs and anti-establishmentism with a vindictive Puritan streak which liked to see neighbours discomfited. A good example of the tone was a list of recommended targets for April Fool's published by the *American Magazine of Useful Knowledge* in 1835: the idle, the profligate, people who had married for 'the wrong reasons', the thickos. It commented: 'Though our own individual follies are too intimately blended with our natures to be seen or felt, yet the dullest of us are sufficiently acute in detecting the foolery of our neighbors.'

Barnum, whose father was a hard-working but ruthless New England store owner, personified this. As one of his obituarists neatly put it, he profited from a strange combination of 'thrift, temperance and misrepresentation on a large scale'. He also loved April Fool's. Although his world was so full of fakery that an actual prank on April the first must have been difficult to detect from the general air of deceit, he insisted on carrying out the annual ritual. In 1851, for instance, he was in Nashville, Tennessee, running a promotional tour by the singer Jenny Lind. He set aside the whole afternoon for fooling, ordering a stack of telegraph forms which he sent to friends and family with what a friend called 'messages full of the most sensational and startling intelligence' or spurious invitations to attractions such as the Great Exhibition which had just opened in London's Crystal Palace. Even his daughter, who was helping with the tour, was a victim. Barnum watched her hurry off in response to one of his telegrams which said that her mother, cousin and several other relatives were waiting for her at a neighbouring town. They weren't. He then spent a happy evening reading puzzled replies from his targets, wired back to his hotel.

All good fun maybe. But the influence of Barnum, Day, Gordon Bennett and the other wholesale liars in the media gradually came to worry some of the US's leading thinkers. Herman Melville set his last novel, *The Confidence Man*, entirely on April Fool's Day and published it on the first of April, in 1857, to press home the point. It was a sombre look at the vices encompassed by the American speciality of 'smart dealing', the technique taught so well to Phineas Barnum by his father. The devil boards a Mississippi riverboat and tries to dupe his fellow passengers, representatives of gullible Americans prone to the tricks of charlatans because they were always after easy money. The novel was well reviewed in Europe but the New York press recognised that their abandonment of truth was part of the target, and bit back. 'Such puerilities will sell, of course, because Mr. Melville wrote them,' said the *New York Dispatch*. 'But this exceedingly talented author must beware, or he will tire out the patience of his readers.'

Melville's point struck home, however, and helped to begin a long, slow transformation of the worst in the American newspapers, parallel with other reforms and changing attitudes which placed some limits on the excessively 'smart'. It didn't happen overnight. From the 1890s until the mid-20th century the poisonous William Randolph Hearst filled his papers with lies for political and often maliciously personal reasons. He went to bizarre lengths such as running a photograph in 1932 of 'the unemployed storming Buckingham Palace' which was actually taken of anxious crowds waiting for news about King George V when he was seriously ill three years earlier. Amid this venom, sweet little April Fool's japes such as the Toronto *Mail and Empire*'s discovery of a golden typewriter in the tomb of Tutankhamun passed relatively unnoticed (although rivals guilelessly followed it up by interviewing leading but baffled Egyptologists).

In the end, it was Hearst's nemesis Orson Welles who dealt transatlantic hoaxing a deadly blow. Years before *Citizen Kane* used the greater power of film to expose the Hearst empire, Welles created one of the United States' biggest ever panics. In 1938 he used his exceptional acting skills to make a modernised, radio version of H.G. Wells's *War of the Worlds*, setting the Martian invasion in New Jersey and reporting the aliens' progress in realistic news bulletins. Thousands of people in New York fled their homes, hospitals were overwhelmed with shock victims, armed citizens headed for the supposed battle-fields and prayer meetings were held across the country. Hoaxers everywhere were given pause by this demonstration of how spoofs in the hands of the new and truly mass media could have a disastrous effect. Today, American journalism is almost excessively virtuous in its attitudes to accuracy and trying to paint a truthful picture of complex and fast-moving events. But fortunately April Fool's has survived this imposition of good behaviour. On one day a year, they remind us of the wild old days of life on the moon and nannies who lived for 161 years.

A M E R I C A N   P L A Y

A DANGEROUS DAY

On April Fool's Day in 1838 an American teen called Rebecca Bullard wrote to her brother John in Hopkinton, Massachusetts, giving an excellent picture of pranks at her boarding school in Boston. Punctuation wasn't a strong suit for teenagers btw, then as now.

Dear Brother,

It is the first day of April + it is impossible to do anything there has been nothing but fooling done. We comenced before day + have kept it up all day in the first place L Inglis went to her brothers door + told them that something had happened to Dr Warren + they must go directly + see him they both dressed then + come down in the greatest hurry when we all ran after them + cried (le poisson d Avril) or April fool then Emma Beatman took the bell + went up into the hall + rang for prayers. We all scampered up stairs + who should be there but Emma laughing ready to kill herself at our foolishness. However she was paid for it for a couple of the girls took a large box + filled it with rags nailed it up + carried it into the kitchen + got one of the kitchen girls to com in in the middle of school + say that there was a box Emma delighted ran down burst open the box + found that it was just a civil return upon her. Others have received letters but no name to them. Maria Fay received a love letter most beautifully written she really thought she

knew who it was from after she had gloried over it long enough Miss
James told her that Miss Derby wrote it that she got her too. Miss
Brooks received one had to pay ten cents + there was nothing but a
blank piece of paper. I have been really afraid to move.

GREEDY, GREEDY

Right at the time in the 1840s when European visitors were
denouncing American greed for a fast buck, an April Fool by the *Boston
Post* proved their point. It electrified the city by announcing that a
cavern full of gold, jewels and other loot had been found by workmen
digging out the roots of a felled tree on Boston Common. One of the
men's pickaxes rang on a stone trapdoor which proved to be set with
an iron ring. Heave-ho. The secret entrance to a flight of steps was
revealed – and everyone could go and have a peek at the presumed
pirate hoard or cache left by the dastardly British on April the first. As
an eyewitness recorded: 'It was rainy, the Legislature was in session,
and it was an animated scene that the Common presented, roofed
with umbrellas, sheltering pilgrims on their way. A procession of
grave legislators marched solemnly down under their green gingham
with philosophers, archaeologists, numismatists, antiquarians of all
qualities, and the public.' Nothing awaited them except disappointment, the rain-soaked turf of the common and a small hole. And the
Boston Post saying 'April Fool.'

GETTING THE PICTURE

An unusually elegant pictorial guide to American April Fool's was
published by *Harper's Weekly* to mark the day in 1864. Like some of the
more ludicrous but ingeniously compiled hoaxes which have been
played since, it was not intended to deceive anyone but to show the
range of pranks in vogue. Packed with detail, the engraving by Thomas
Nast shows women donning beards and moustaches, soldiers serving in
the Civil War (then raging) blocking colleagues' views by putting their
hands over binoculars, a little boy tying a girl's dress strings without her
noticing and – joyous perennial – an absent-minded schoolteacher with
a sign reading 'Old Fool' pinned to his back. The cartoon served a more
serious political purpose by mocking over-optimistic military

announcements, another feature of life which has not changed. A bill claiming the fall of Richmond, the Confederate capital, was a direct dig at the unreliable coverage of the *New York Tribune*. A meeting of geese and donkeys meanwhile guyed the 'Copperhead' faction of the Democratic Party which favoured a negotiated peace with the rebels.

THE GREAT INVENTOR

The brilliant but ruthless inventor Thomas Edison was credited with almost magical powers by late-19th-century Americans. What he couldn't dream up himself, he stole from others. So the *New York Graphic* pitched at just the right level in its 1878 April Fool which revealed that Edison had come up with a machine which could turn soil instantly into cereal crops. No more boring sowing and growing – although the Great Plains prairies must have seen some farmers have heart attacks when the scoop was passed on. Passed on it was. Hundreds of credulous local papers reprinted the news, adding that the food machine could also turn water into wine. This biblical touch increased the celebrations of a generally devout nation until the *Graphic* confessed its spoof. It did this elegantly by reproducing a particularly gushing leading article on Edison's food machine in the *Buffalo Commercial Advertiser* under the brief headline: 'They Bite'.

MISSING A DEAL

It isn't like Americans to miss a bargain but nearly 60,000 people in Boston lost out on an April Fool's deal in 1915. Their paper the *Boston Globe* appeared on April the first with its cover price reduced by half to just one cent. The change wasn't flagged, simply altered in the usual spot below the masthead and above the columns of advertisements. Nobody gave that half a glance because they were so used to it. The editor and business staff didn't know about it either, until with the shops almost empty of copies, someone insisted on getting the new price. The prankster was a printer who slipped in a new line of type at the last minute. He was soon employed elsewhere.

SEE-THROUGH COZZIES

It was an American correspondent who broke the news of the briefly notorious dissolving swimming costumes which seemed to sum up the decadence of the European rich in the 1920s. Readers were told how a British millionaire on the French Riviera gave his guests the stylish swimwear which then gradually dissolved in the salt water with which he filled his pool. There was historical backing for this in tales from the Beau Nash era in Bath when women were sometimes tricked into wearing thin cotton costumes for the spa which became transparent after several minutes underwater. The problem for the reporter who made up the story was that his bosses back in the States wanted some of the stunt cozzies to show readers. His ingenious get-out was to grind a box of muesli into fine dust and ship it across the Atlantic in a sealed box. Despite the airproof lining, his colleagues concluded when they tore this open, salt air had got at the precious consignment and ruined it.

CAPITAL FUN

The picture desk on the *Madison Capital-Times* took, and deserved, most of the credit for the paper's April Fool in 1933 which dramatically showed the Wisconsin State Capitol building tumbling over like a classical Humpty-Dumpty. The image was everything, although the accompanying story had all the usual features of an April Fool – a complicated farrago about an explosion caused by an accumulation of political hot air. Or as the writers put it: 'large quantities of gas, generated through many weeks of verbose debate in the Senate and Assembly chambers'. As well as credit for pulling the wool, the *Capital-Times* picture editor also had to shoulder his share of blame. Many readers were outraged, one describing the spoof as 'not only tactless and void of humor, but also a hideous jest'.

SPOIL SPORTS

April Fools were a speciality for many years at the *Honolulu Star-Bulletin*, whose triumphs included the discovery of a Viking explorer's ship in 1936 (nicely anticipating Thor Heyerdahl's Kon Tiki expedition by eleven years) and the catching of the world's biggest fish three years later. These pranks involved the paper's staff in heroic DIY as the amazing objects were actually constructed for photographs to be taken

The collapsing dome of the Wisconsin State Capitol at Madison, 1 April 1933.

and in the case of the fish to be paraded around Hawaii on a lorry float. The paper took umbrage, however, when its rivals at the islands' radio station outdid all the wacky creations with a simple April Fool. A bulletin on the US Congress passing the Hawaii statehood bill added that when the islands joined the Union, all federal income tax paid during the previous year would be refunded. The people of Hawaii went wild first with joy and then with anger when they discovered that they had been had. The *Star-Bulletin* piously announced that it was ending its own tradition of spoofs in sympathy with them.

HOW DIM CAN YOU BE?

Anyone who believes anything announced on April the first without checking is asking for trouble. So maybe the fact that the Franklin Institute in Philadelphia chose 31 March in 1940 to reveal that the world would end the following morning lulled people into credulity. Whatever, the hardened hacks at the city's Radio KYW broadcast this urgent announcement: 'Your worst fears that the world will end are confirmed by astronomers of Franklin Institute, Philadelphia. Scientists predict that the world will end at 3 P.M. Eastern Standard Time tomorrow. This is no April Fool joke. Confirmation can be obtained from Wagner Schlesinger, director of the Fels Planetarium of this city.' Panic duly followed until repeated reassurances from the Franklin, a highly respected scientific research centre and museum named after the illustrious Benjamin. Their denials were genuine. The prank was played on his own initiative and without consulting anyone by the institute's press agent William Castellini, who was sacked shortly afterwards. Poor chap. He had only wanted to get a good audience for a genuine lecture at the museum by Mr Schlesinger on 1 April entitled 'How the world will end'.

VIRGINIA WOOLF AND HER FEBRUARY FOOL

Mention the name of the writer Virginia Woolf and most people will think of an angular and pallid neurotic who took her own life by drowning in a Sussex river which looks more like a drain. This makes a set of photographs of the Emperor of Abyssinia's visit to London in 1910 that much more extraordinary. On the left sits a young Ethiopian nobleman with chiselled features and a fine beard and moustache. He is described as Prince Mendax but he is actually Virginia Woolf.

Daubed in brown greasepaint from Clarkson's, the leading theatrical costumiers of the day, she formed part of the retinue of the fictitious 'Emperor' – actually an Old Harrovian athlete called Anthony Buxton – who managed to cod the Royal Navy into laying on a guided tour of HMS *Dreadnought*, the pride of the world's greatest fleet.

The *Dreadnought* hoax: left to right: Virginia Woolf, Duncan Grant, Adrian Stephen, Anthony Buxton as the Emperor of Abyssinia, Guy Ridley, Horace Cole. *Mary Evans*

Murmuring phrases such as 'Bunga bunga' and 'Chuck-a-choi', the hoaxers were conducted all over the partly secret battleship, regaled with the Zanzibari national anthem (because the Royal Marines band had no music for the Abyssinian one) and offered a 21-gun salute.

Woolf was addressing envelopes for the National Union of Women's Suffrage Societies when, at two days' notice, she was offered a part in this most audacious of April Fool's. Actually it was a February Fool because its prime instigator, a Cambridge graduate called Horace de Vere Cole who had plenty of money and time on his hands, felt that fixing the stunt for 1 April would be taking one risk too many.

Cole had become a sort-of professional April Fooler after getting to know Woolf's brother Adrian Stephen at Cambridge, where the great hoax was hatched for the most mundane of reasons: a spell of boredom in the life of clever but underoccupied people. Similar feelings have underlain a great many more of the other hoaxes in this book; an urge to spice life up a bit and in Stephen's words 'to pull the leg of anyone who took up an attitude of authority over anyone else'.

Showing a touch of the madness which ran in his family, Stephen first suggested to Cole in his rooms at Trinity College that the pair of them should dress up as German officers and lead a detachment of the Kaiser's army across the highly sensitive border of Alsace-Lorraine. Stephen recalled: 'There would, I hoped, have been what is called an "international incident", the Kaiser would have made gestures and sent telegrams, and other people might have been amused.' On the other hand, the First World War might have broken out five years earlier than it eventually did.

Cole came up with a less incendiary alternative which was also cheaper and more practical. He and Stephen, along with three student friends, donned make-up, beards and turbans and impersonated the Sultan of Zanzibar (who was visiting London at the time) for an official visit to Cambridge. Cole pretended to be the Sultan's bilingual uncle and managed to tour his own college where he passed unrecognised before attending a mayoral reception in the Guildhall and then a charity bazaar where, according to Stephen, the party did at least make 'enormous purchases at all the stalls'. There was one moment of the sort of danger which the pranksters relished when a retired woman missionary asked to speak to the Sultan in Swahili. Cole explained that no woman could address the Exalted One unless she was willing to join his harem.

The Cambridge caper had the desired effect of tweaking authority's tail. The mayor tried to get the culprits sent down from the university (or expelled) and there was widespread newspaper coverage, which gratified Cole's desire for fame. The *Dreadnought* Hoax was a natural follow-on, with the added spice of pulling a really big leg. By 1910, the false foreigners had become more political, albeit in the cavalier way of wealthy dissidents, and the trip to the ship had everything required of a day of misrule. They were cheeking the Empire, mocking its most elaborate security, exposing fusty bureaucrats and dressing up. Indeed, there was the frisson of cross-dressing. Two of the party, Stephen and the artist Duncan Grant (who played another bearded noble), were gay partners. The group also knew that they were aiming to hit the establishment where it hurt. The Cambridge hoax had been accepted in 'society', Stephen admitted honestly, because the mayor was 'only a Cambridge tradesman (he kept a chemist's shop) whereas naval officers, as one critic later said, were "different" – they were "men of honour"'.

To the hoaxers, this made them all the more necessary to bamboozle. Disguised by Clarkson, the group caught an express train to Weymouth where the *Dreadnought* lay at anchor with – added incentive for Woolf and Stephen – their somewhat pompous cousin Commander William Fisher serving in a senior position on board. Like them, he had been given a classical education and it would be all the more wonderful if he not only failed to unmask familiar relatives, one a woman disguised as a man and the other standing a distinctive 6ft 5 ins tall, but didn't pick up the clue in Virginia's false name, Mendax. It means 'liar' in Latin. Cole, who was impersonating a deaf official from the Foreign Office, meanwhile sent a fake telegram to the ship from his superior, apologising for the short notice of the visit, and en route mugged up basic Swahili with Stephen from a phrasebook published by the Society for the Propagation of the Gospel.

They were met with a red carpet at Weymouth station, a saluting officer and a brass-funnelled launch which sped them to the battleship, bedecked with flags. Unrecognised by Fisher and another officer who belonged to Stephen's weekend walking club, they toured the ship for several hours. Early on, the Swahili broke down but Stephen and Cole improvised brilliantly with Chapter 4 of Virgil's *Aeneid*, with the stress broken up, and a little Homer. When Grant's moustache came loose in drizzle on deck, Stephen said that the visitors were suffering from the cold and on the way inside managed to dab the false whiskers back into place.

It was a remarkable escapade, topped and tailed when another naval launch cut across the bows of the Imperial party on their return to shore, breaching etiquette (another target for leg-pulling) and earning a reprimand for its skipper who was a junior member of the British royal family. Back in London, the group agreed that the stunt was perfect in itself and should not be publicised, particularly as the Navy had proved so charming and kind. Cole however needed his cleverness to be known and went to the newspapers. The story was a sensation for a fortnight, with anger in Parliament, a half-cock revenge by naval officers who kidnapped Grant but couldn't (as 'men of honour') bring themselves to duff him up, and much interest in Virginia. She was described in the *Daily Express* as 'very good-looking, with classical features' in spite of her facial hair. She later incorporated the prank in *Orlando*, several short stories and a paper she gave in 1940 to the Women's Institute in Rodmell, the Sussex village where she killed herself a year later.

There are two interesting lessons for April Foolers in the story: the self-confidence which carried the stunt off and the character of its main organiser, de Vere Cole. All the participants were wealthy and accustomed to getting their own way and as Stephen said afterwards, they took command of the situation naturally, even when dealing with an admiral and his officers. 'By the time we reached the *Dreadnought*, it was hardly a question any longer of a hoax,' he said. 'We were almost acting the truth. Everyone was expecting us to act as the Emperor and his suite, and it would have been exceedingly difficult not to.'

Cole meanwhile showed the manic best and worst of the fooling genius. He could not restrain the hoaxing impulse, nor the need to tell everyone about it. Even on his honeymoon he organised small piles of horse dung in the Piazza San Marco in Venice to make it look as though the bronze chargers on the façade of St Mark's cathedral had been out early on April Fool's Day and got caught short. No one was surprised when his wife sued for an early divorce. But although his pranks included old chestnuts, such as persuading a passer-by to hold one end of a length of string and then disappearing round the corner and giving the other end to someone else picked at random, he had exceptionally original ideas. He organised a supper for a group of strangers who discovered during introductions that their surnames all included the word 'bottom'. He booked two rows at a theatre for bald men, an innocuous gathering until they took their seats.

Alas, his endless jokes and publicity-seeking wore out his friends as well as his family. He lost money in unwise investments, his second wife had an embarrassingly public fling with Augustus John and he retired to France where he felt an exile, never at home. Only in very recent times did the joking return. A Yale University professor and authority on hoaxes, Wes Davis, records 'the normally restrained *Dictionary of National Biography*' as describing the old jester in a pitiful state before his death in 1936. 'His advanced deafness prevented him from realising that his carefully timed coughing was inadequate to cover his explosive breaking of wind.' Search the *DNB* and you will find such an entry. Note too the date of publication of the professor's article on the Globalist Foundation website: 1 April last year. Long after his death, the ghost of Cole must have allowed itself a smile.

3

Formula for a Fool

Facts are common to all; but fancies are common only among rare souls and those touched with a certain quality of genius.

ETHELREDA LEWIS, 1875–1946, AUTHOR (AND INVENTOR) OF *TRADER HORN*

*i*T IS PROBABLY TRUE THAT SOME PEOPLE ARE BORN APRIL FOOLERS AND THAT OTHERS HAVE SPOOFERY THRUST UPON THEM. But there is also a reputable school of thought which holds that successful practical jokes can be taught and learned. One of its leading gurus was Professor Reginald Victor Jones, a distinguished physicist whose trickery with radar and deception in the Second World War played an important part in the air defence of Britain.

Jones was a serious scientist with many other achievements to his name, but he had a lifelong relish for playing tricks. As a student he perfected the Telephone Repair Joke which is so long-drawn-out that describing it in writing would be tedious. But it essentially involves a fake phone service official taking a subscriber through a series of tests of supposedly faulty equipment which end with the instruction to place the receiver in a basin of water. Jones kept a tally of the number of PhDs at Cambridge whom he gulled into doing this. The joke depended partly on Jones's particular ability to impersonate a GPO official but it also had a practical, scientific basis. The victim's belief that something really was wrong with their phone was encouraged by

Jones repeatedly ringing them and then putting down the receiver as soon as they answered.

In 1957 Jones gave a lecture which was published soon afterwards in the *Bulletin of the Institute of Physics* on the subject of 'The theory of practical joking – its relevance to physics'. He set out a number of rules which form the framework of a successful prank: for example, the production of incongruity into the normal course of events. Refining this for the best jokes, the arrival of something odd had to be preceded by an 'induction' as in the case of the abortive phone calls. Jones gave two examples of fiendishly contrived April Fool's, one involving an apparently magic television and the other a pet tortoise.

The TV prank was carried out in 1934 by a German physicist, Dr Carl Bosch, whose flat overlooked the home of a local journalist. Pretending to be his own professor at the university, Bosch phoned this newspaperman to announce that he had perfected a form of videophone which could see what the recipient was doing. The journalist was sceptical but Bosch suggested an experiment: the man was to strike a series of poses and the voice on the phone would describe what he was doing. Unaware that the 'professor' could see him from his flat above, the journalist capered about. The voice on the phone duly described every movement. Two days later, the local paper headlined this astonishing breakthrough, much to the surprise of Bosch's true professor who had a subsequent conversation with the reporter and his editor which left all three of them bewildered.

Jones liked to add that he had fooled this particular fooler himself. His secret war at one stage involved spreading disinformation about British ships and planes detecting German U-boats with an infrared ray. The Nazis wasted months designing an anti-infrared paint which was then applied to all the U-boats, taking many of them out of action for vital weeks. The paint was designed by the spoofer Bosch, and it was very clever, Jones said. It was also pointless because the submarines were actually being detected by secret sonar.

The tortoise joke was even more ingenious than the videophone. It also involved a flat, but this time in Paris, where another physicist (a class unusually prone to japes, as Jones remarks in his paper) lived above a woman with a pet tortoise. The scientist, a Dr R.W. Wood, embarked on a bizarre deception. He bought a collection of tortoises of different sizes and then, when his neighbour was out, started substituting them for her pet, using a home-made net like a butterfly collector's which reached into her garden. Every day, he replaced the tortoise with a slightly bigger one until the apparent growth of her pet was so dramatic that the woman went first to a zoology professor at the Sorbonne and then to the press. At this point, Wood reversed the process and replaced the tortoises in descending order of size until the original one was safely back with its lettuces. The ploy has since become internationally famous through its use by Roald Dahl as the plot of his children's book *Esio Trot* (practised April Foolsters will need no encouragement to read that title backwards). But whether Dahl read of Dr Wood's prank or thought it up separately is not known. There are no relevant references in the author's literary archive.

Jones enjoyed illustrating the theory of induced incongruity in classes at Aberdeen University, where he was a hugely popular lecturer after the war. His methods included firing a pistol, for which he had won sharpshooting medals at Bisley when a student at Oxford in the 1930s. Dead pigeons fell from the ceiling at appropriate moments. His forceful and self-confident character was also a great help in his deceptions. His wife Vera fell in love with him after he helped her chase off a 'Dad's Army' Home Guard battalion who had started digging air raid trenches on her women's hockey pitch at the Admiralty Research Laboratory in Teddington, Middlesex.

Jones retained his enthusiasm for April Foolery until his death in 1997. He was put in charge of a government inquiry into flying saucers, which greatly delighted him, and he greeted his appointment as head of radar countermeasures in the Second World War with glee. The brief to use as much skullduggery and misleading ploys as possible was a prankster's paradise, he told friends – 'The culmination of all my pre-war efforts at practical joking with virtually as much of the national resources at my disposal as I wish.' Further work on his theory, however, was left to another academic, an American professor of journalism called Curtis MacDougall who immersed himself for years in the theory and practice of hoaxes.

He drew up a list of four reasons why most of us are credulous and seven social and cultural 'incentives' to belief, which an April Fooler should bear in mind. The four curbs on scepticism are indifference – a casual lack of specialised interest in the subject which is being sent up; ignorance and superstition; suggestion, a dark art which cunningly simulates familiar situations and then adds a twist; and prestige, the crucial one for newspapers, broadcasters and websites. If the claims are coming from a Richard Dimbleby, *The Times* or a familiar website, they are very much more likely to be believed.

Most of us also pass our days in a state of good-natured trust which is healthy for ourselves and society – but also a gift to those playing April Fool's jokes. As MacDougall says, belief is 'natural and pleasant' as well as a part of our original innocent natures, as in the belief of children in Father Christmas. It isn't a lazy disinclination to question, however; challenging and checking is necessary, but humanity's progress would have been much slower without the drive of an optimism about our ability to overcome obstacles, a belief that everything is possible.

Thus the prankster starts with an advantage. The incentives he or she can add include financial gain, vanity, promoting a cause, chauvinism, prejudice and pet theories, a thirst for vicarious thrills and finally an appropriate cultural climate: spoofers need to tune their tricks to current issues and the contemporary mood. Ally an understanding of these with Professor Jones's theory of producing an incongruity after an induction, and possibly a thorough reading of the examples in this book, and the secret of success can be yours.

The hope of financial gain figures large in advertisement April Fool's spoofs, many of which offer coupons, phone lines or email addresses for fabulous deals such as *The Times*'s ill-fated world tour at the 19th-century prices charged by the original Thomas Cook (see page 65). Instead of the hoped-for bargain, a little answer comes back saying 'Gotcha' in a variety of ways; or as with Google's regular online hoaxes on 1 April, a reminder of the date and an invitation to try again next year. The chastening archive of suckered victims of buried treasure April Fool's hoaxes also fits with the estimate that every American loses an average of 15 dollars a year to swindlers and con artists. Think of all those greedy Bostonians who turned out in a rainstorm in the 1840s to find the local newspaper's 'pirate hoard', and ended their April the first getting deservedly soaked.

Vanity meanwhile led the all-powerful Royal Navy into the treacherous clutches of Virginia Woolf and her *Dreadnought* team; the hoaxers were helped enormously by their own self-confidence, but it was the almost unbelievable overconfidence of their victims which really saw them through. Step forward also the long line of hood-winked experts, from Athanasius Kircher and the mirror-writing Chinese script hoax to Lord Dacre whose immense prestige as Regius professor of history at Oxford University blinded him to the many flaws in Hitler's supposed diaries, 62 volumes of nonsense created by an impressively dedicated German fraud in 1983.

There was perhaps an element of prejudice and chauvinism which helped undermine Lord Dacre's judgement. Certainly we can find a stout tradition of April Fool's based on attitudes to foreigners which come so naturally, especially in 19th- and 20th-century Britain, that they can remain unspoken. The prankster's mind and his victim's naturally click together. Hence *The Times*'s abolition of Belgium and *The Independent*'s discovery of the remains of Asterix the Gaul's original village, with the latter joke also using the 'prestige' incentive to credulity by enlisting genuine archaeologists in the scheme. Excessive national pride can be as much of a trap as mocking the foreigner; there is a long roll-call of 'genuine' Gaelic romances such as Ossian the non-existent bard, ancient British discoveries of electricity or the helicopter and American dragon bones which citizens of the respective countries very much want to believe and therefore do.

There is a dark side to this desire to believe too, exploited by April Fool's which play on the stuff of nightmares. Orson Welles' radio production of *The War of the Worlds* showed the potential power of this genre, but on a more homely level it accounted for the widespread belief when the *Guardian* revealed Peter Mandelson's appointment as chairman of the BBC on 1 April 2004. This was the stuff of night-mares, especially within Broadcasting House where the spoof had many of its most credulous victims. The *Guardian* tilled the same furrow last year with its revelation that Chris Martin of Coldplay was supporting new Tory Boy David Cameron with a special record. Those most immediately hooked were the spinners at Labour Party headquarters, who had woken up sweating in the past after bad dreams about exactly this sort of 'cool' endorsement of their main and still somewhat inscrutable rival.

Both those spoofs were also linked to events in the headlines at the time; and subverting the current cultural climate is the most effective April Fool incentive to credulity of all. It has played a part in all the Great Fools such as the BBC *Panorama* spaghetti harvest of 1957, which would not succeed in today's much more knowing culinary times and without the central, august personage of a Richard Dimbleby to overawe doubters. The technique was also central to the timing of San Serriffe, published by the *Guardian* in 1977 during a period when newspaper supplements on little-known countries were as much a part of British life as vagueness about the '-stan' countries of Central Asia was when Sacha Baron Cohen invented his monstrously successful Kazakh journalist Borat in the late 1990s. Another fine example was what we might call the Great White Hoax played in the *Guardian* in the early 1970s by Martin Kemp, an academic at Glasgow University who is now the Professor of the History of Art at Oxford.

Kemp knew his art history very well even back in Harold Wilson's day and he was also abreast of the modish whims of the contemporary art world which have since made the Turner Prize such an annual source of joy. In cahoots with the *Guardian*'s art editor Mike McNay, another knowledgeable monitor of the gallery scene, he wrote a short but enthusiastic review of a Young Turk artist who had filled an entire gallery in the Scottish town of Auchtermuchty (previously little known at the cutting edge of art) with blank white canvases, thereby expressing several supposedly important ideas about Art to which Kemp paid homage. It was a convincing Fool. *Guardian* readers mostly took it at face value and McNay still winces as he recalls fielding phone calls from enthusiastic art lovers who wanted details of the gallery's address and the exhibition dates. They were disappointed and in some cases very cross to be told that they were victims of a joke.

Kemp was well schooled in academic April Foolery. As a student at the Courtauld Institute in London he drew up plans for an entirely spoof edition of the prestigious *Burlington Magazine* which sadly remained unrealised because of the cost. He had also learned a little of the more basic side of hoaxing while lecturing on Prince Edward Island in Canada where, he recalls, the newspaper ran the same April Fool every year. 'The capital St John's has a very narrow harbour entrance and they always published a photograph of a stray iceberg blocking it – which would mean economic ruin. One year they dropped it and there was a tremendous protest from readers because the joke had become an institution. Locals liked knowing that there'd always be the odd newcomer or visitor who fell for it, which was certainly the case with me.'

Kemp's expertise with an academic Fool which also carried popular, gut appeal was matched by the equally scholarly Philip French in 1990. Feeling frolicsome, he added a modestly untrumpeted paragraph to his weekly film criticism for *The Observer* on 1 April mentioning that the original version of Orson Welles' masterpiece *The Magnificent Ambersons* had finally been re-assembled and was being shown at the National Film Theatre later in the week. This is a Holy Grail for film enthusiasts; Welles' original rough cut in 1942 was altered during his absence in Brazil against his wishes by Robert Wise who later went on to direct *The Sound of Music*. The only copy of the original was supposedly sent to Welles but disappeared. Now, apparently, it had been found. Within hours the writer Julian Barnes, who lived in a neighbouring street in Hampstead, was excitedly asking French's wife, whom he met on a Sunday morning stroll, for more details. The NFT was bombarded with ticket requests and excitement spiralled, until the next Sunday French had to add a footnote to his column saying: didn't you notice the date? It was a classic of the April Fool succeeding because well-chosen victims desperately wanted to believe that it was true.

French acknowledges the influence of another successful spoofer, his friend and colleague Gilbert Adair, whose flight of fancy in *Sight and Sound* magazine is gradually becoming a sort of truth. Adair celebrated April Fool's Day in 1987 with a piece about the critic and philosopher Roland Barthes and his admiration for the *Carry On* films, whose insights the heavyweight French intellectual described in

convincingly sociological terms. Hattie Jacques, Kenneth Williams &
Co were playing at being doctors, nurses and so forth in much the way
children do, the Frenchman concluded, as have many humbler
minds.

> Not unexpectedly [wrote Barthes/Adair], the common denominator
> turns out to be the bedpan, a Grail-like receptacle for the *Carry On*
> scenarists, whose almost too obvious analogy is with the 'potty'. Thus
> the eroticism of the series has jammed at the fundamentally infantile
> stage of disclosure, in which nudity is a (never quite attained)
> culmination, rather than a point of departure.

Among many repetitions of this fantasy which remain uncorrected
and reproduce endlessly on the internet is a long interview with
another *Carry On* star, Barbara Windsor, which was published in the
Guardian in 1990. In it, Suzanne Moore describes Barthes more
accurately than she knew as 'perhaps the most unlikely admirer of the
Carry On films.'

Some years later a more elaborate version of these artistic follies
successfully ambushed the art world itself, rather than merely duping
enthusiastic gallery-goers. The novelist William Boyd got together
with the artist Jeff Koons and singer and actor David Bowie to
construct a fascinating but non-existent painter called Nat Tate. A
short but devastating biography was launched on April Fool's Day
1998 at a gallery in New York, much of which took this new and tragic
hero to its heart. Tate was an orphan, whose struggle for recognition
as 'an abstract impressionist notionally of the New York School' was
vividly recounted by Boyd. The painter's friendship with Picasso and
Braque had helped to bring him recognition but not as much as a love
affair with Peggy Guggenheim. Tragically, this was short-lived. After
destroying all his work at the age of 31, Tate (whose name was an
amalgam of Britain's two best-known galleries, the National and the
Tate) caught the Staten Island ferry in 1960, climbed on to the
railings at the stern and threw himself into New York harbour. His
body, of course, was never found.

The book's cover featured a photo of the smouldering but mentally tortured young artist and on the back Gore Vidal, who was also in on the hoax, summed him up as 'essentially dignified, drunk with nothing to say.' It won such endorsements as 'a beautifully penned glimpse of greatness.' It was then exposed, by arrangement, in the *New York Times* and *The Independent* in London and there were many red faces, especially in commercial galleries which had started a hunt for three supposedly surviving Tate works. Some said that the prank exposed the shallow greed of New York's art market. Others that it was intended simply as a work of art in itself. The book was later reprinted, sold well and has since been described by several critics as Boyd's best attempt at fiction.

Ironically, similar outlandish galleries, exhibitions and artists have since happened genuinely; and there is a final side to April Fool's psychology which brings together – almost – those old contenders illusion and reality. One of the oldest techniques of the pranksters, much in evidence on the internet's innumerable pages of online spoofs, is interminable technical detail. This follows in a tradition of technobabble surrounding the inventions of, for instance, the annual BMW car improvement gadget April Fool's, or the cruder jokes of the 19th- and early 20th-century American press with their faked photographs of public buildings collapsing or peculiar creatures found in remote forests or archaeologists' excavations.

One particularly fine example of laborious but worthwhile attention to detail was the Upside-Down Library Fool organised by the BBC teatime programme *Nationwide* in 1976. The thesis was simple but implausible: the model town of Milton Keynes, which had just embarked genuinely on a £100 million improvement of its civic centre, had mistakenly built its new library upside down because plans had been photocopied the wrong way up. To enhance the idea's teetering credibility, the TV people went to town. The reporter Martin Young interviewed a harassed librarian as the pair of them walked round the building, circumventing light fittings sticking up from the floor. Books tumbled from shelves, an Irish builder (this was 30 years ago, remember) explained that he had simply followed the plans. A man from the council blamed the architect and the architect refused to comment. It made five and a half minutes of very well-

TEN WHOLESOME PRANKS

☺ **Make** an apple-pie bed by folding the sheet back up, tucking it in tightly and encouraging your child/spouse/friend to jump in vigorously.

☺ **Balance** a pillow on top of a slightly open door.

☺ **Turn** the clocks an hour back.

☺ **Carefully** unroll the lavatory paper for a couple of feet and write 'Help! I am a prisoner in a lavatory paper factory' on one sheet.

☺ **Take** a universal remote control into one of those mass TV sales stores and turn the volume to maximum.

☺ **Sneak** an adhesive Post-it note under a colleague's computer mouse to disable it (writing 'April Fool' on the note first).

☺ **Switch** the signs for men's and ladies lavatories in the office.

☺ **Unscrew** all toothpaste tubes and slide in a raisin.

☺ **Add** quick-acting dry yeast to pancake mix, then ask mum/wife/friend to cook pancakes for lunch or dinner. Stand well back.

☺ **Pour** out cereal and milk and put in freezer overnight. Add dash of milk and a spoonful of cereal in the morning and serve at once.

crafted TV, even if it lacked a Richard Dimbleby to make it immortal. Ho, ho, ho. But time has the last laugh on many of these elaborate spoofs and inventions whose victims were mocked at the time. Some of the world's iconic new buildings unquestionably look as though they have been built upside down; and Dr Carl Bosch's interactive television is now part of all our lives.

I leave the last psychological word to myself, from an undercover week in 1978 when I was admitted to the fringes of a plot which fooled British Rail and credulous journalists with a fake scheme for taking dogs free on the network on one special Sunday. The chief prankster left no detail to chance, paying for his own sumptuous leaflets for the 'Rover' special offer, organising a press release which the Press Association among others swallowed, adding the leaflets to racks at the main London stations and finding a call box at Marylebone whose number was given as the contact for BR's nearby headquarters. In the aftermath, a rail official was quoted by the *Daily Telegraph* as saying: 'I can't understand why people should go to such expense.' But that was ironically part of the reason. To read such comments in the papers and witness, yet again, the credulity of the media as well as its customers gave the fooler and his posse a warm glow. The *Telegraph* report ended by saying that 'details are being given to British Transport Police today'. But nearly 30 years is such a long time, and my memory is not what it was, so I would no longer be able to be of assistance to their enquiries.

4

Spaghetti Doesn't Grow on Trees

No man is lonely eating spaghetti; it requires so much attention.

CHRISTOPHER MORLEY, 1890–1957, US AUTHOR AND JOURNALIST

SOMEWHERE IN AN ATTIC OR A TRUNK THERE MAY BE 7.92 METRES OF BRITTLE, CENTURY-OLD CELLULOID WHICH RECORDS THE FIRST APRIL FOOL TO MAKE IT INTO FILM. Made in 1902 and called *Dan Leno and Herbert Campbell edit The Sun*, it shows the two Victorian comedians in an obviously fake newspaper office plagued by simple gags such as spilling ink and losing pens. The film re-created an actual event. Campbell and Leno, who were the greatest music hall draw of the day, were invited to edit the real *Sun* newspaper in London on 1 April that year, an event with all sorts of modern resonances. The Victorian *Sun* was a very different animal from its modern namesake, but similar creative sparks clearly occupied its Bright Ideas department.

The film was shown across the world sporadically for years and its audiences may well have included a lively young man, originally from Vienna, called Charles de Jaeger. He had a private reason for enjoying the work of Herbert Campbell. The comedian's name meant one thing to most of his fans and that was spaghetti. Campbell's tour de force on stage was a lecture on the correct way to eat spaghetti, a novelty food in Victorian times. He tried forks, spoon, knives and his fingers. He slurped, bit, gagged and spattered his surroundings with tomato sauce. If de Jaeger saw the performance, it is one he would not have forgotten; because spaghetti was twined round his heart.

This dated back to his schooldays in Austria when a humorous but sometimes exasperated teacher used to tell his class: 'Boys, you are so stupid, you'd believe me if I told you that spaghetti grew on trees.' The sally always got a laugh and the thought stayed with young Charles as he went through the school and then talked his way into a job in journalism. He wanted to be at the forefront of things and the cutting-edge medium at the time, in the early 1930s, was film. De Jaeger became a freelance film photographer who was also able to write.

The rise of Hitler saw him flee with many others to Britain where he worked initially for the film unit of General Charles de Gaulle's Free French forces before joining the BBC in 1943. A big, commanding presence, he was soon a well-known figure at major events. He was the first of the corporation's newsreel cameramen to work abroad and he liked to claim one of the pithiest interviews ever given by that great orator Sir Winston Churchill. 'Will you say a few words about what you are going to do?' Charles asked the then Prime Minister as he boarded a plane for talks in Paris. 'I know what I am going to do, young man,' said Churchill. 'I am going to Paris for talks.'

De Jaeger was more successful when he teased the Vatican after his attempts to get a papal audience in the late 1940s proved troublesome. Besieged in English, Italian, French and German, in all of which Charles was fluent, the priests finally said: 'Very well, His Holiness will see you on Tuesday afternoon.' De Jaeger couldn't help countering: 'Yes, but is he a man of his word?' In between film assignments he worked as a researcher for the writer John Gunther on his book *Inside Europe Today* which was a classic study of its time. That showed how serious he could be when required, but those who worked with him recall much more his sense of fun.

This jovial character was one of two men who knocked on the

Panorama's unveiling of the bucolic Swiss spaghetti harvest, its picturesque tradition unchanged over so many generations. *BBC*

office door of Michael Peacock, the editor of BBC TV's flagship programme *Panorama*, early in 1957. The other was a clever young producer called David Wheeler who had earned a name for excellent short films in all the varied fields which *Panorama* had covered since its revamp, from an older but rather feeble version, in September 1955.

Television was limited in those days to one BBC and one ITV channel and it was possible for a programme to hold the nation's attention in a way inconceivable nowadays. *Panorama* was the outstanding example. Its eight to ten million viewers slaughtered ITV's rival offering on Monday evenings, *Wagon Train*. It examined a mixture of subjects, complex and simple, heavy and light, with an air of absolute authority which owed much to its very bright staff but most to the presenter, Richard Dimbleby. A heavyweight in every sense, the father of today's stars David and Jonathan combined the cleverness and fluency of his sons with an almost Prime Ministerial presence. His career dated back to an eyewitness radio account of the Crystal Palace fire in 1936 and by the mid-1950s he was always BBC TV's commentator on state occasions – Parliamentary, royal or first-division events such as the Festival of Britain. It was a common quip after the televised coronation of the present Queen in 1953 that many viewers thought that Dimbleby, rather than the Archbishop of Canterbury, was in charge.

As a result his word was trusted, almost revered. Even when he dealt with *Panorama*'s lighter items, the audience could be sure that what they were hearing was true. He combined his gravitas with a genuinely common touch and the avuncular tone of a favourite uncle. Reports on the Soviet invasion of Hungary in 1956 turned the programme into a national institution and Suez fortified its place. As Jonathan Dimbleby says proudly in his biography of his father: 'Not once was the massive authority of Richard Dimbleby's *Panorama* challenged.' De Jaeger and Wheeler's reason for calling on Peacock was therefore no small matter. They were asking him to persuade a titan of rectitude to lie.

'They made their pitch to me,' Peacock recalls today. 'April 1st would be on a Monday that year – *Panorama* always went out on a Monday night – so this would be a rare opportunity to carry an April

Fool. Charles and David outlined how the story of the spaghetti harvest would go. Charles, a freelance who'd worked for *Panorama* from the start, explained that he was going to be filming in Switzerland anyway. He knew a small village where the women would be happy to take part, and he was sure they could attach spaghetti to trees . . .! So it wouldn't cost much to film the item. They stood there, looking at me expectantly.'

For de Jaeger especially it was a long moment. His friends knew that his teacher's joke had bubbled up regularly from the back of his mind. He had always thought about turning it into a deadpan spoof and had tried several times in his Austrian and German days and at least twice since joining the BBC. With Wheeler on board and enthused, this was much his best chance.

They weren't kept in suspense for long. Peacock says now: 'I couldn't say no. I gave Charles a budget of £100, and off he went. He did a splendid job of filming the harvest, but not enough credit has been given over the years to David Wheeler for the brilliant pastiche newsreel commentary he wrote for Richard Dimbleby.'

That's coming. But Wheeler's work had to wait while de Jaeger scooted round to the Swiss Tourist Office, later to become famous as London's prime cheese and fondue eaterie in the 'Swinging Sixties', whose staff eagerly joined in the fun. They were so enthused that Charles had to swear them to silence before catching a plane to Lugano and an area of picturesque hillside orchards which he knew from previous trips.

'It was in March, when I thought the weather would be sunny with flowers out,' he told Denis Norden in a TV interview many years later. 'But there was a mist over the whole area.' Evidence of this survives in the BBC's written archives at Caversham, just outside Reading. In a file of papers about the spaghetti caper, which includes a list of British pasta manufacturers such as the Busy Bee bakery in Slough, there is a telegram from Lugano's Adler Hotel. Taken down by a Swiss operator whose English was clearly patchy, it is signed with a misspelled 'Jaegar' and says simply 'Wisty weather'. Peacock must have wondered about his £100.

'Then the tourist office guy took me around all over the place,' said de Jaeger. 'Not one blossom out, not even leaves out. Several days went by and it got to the Tuesday before the programme was due. I could not find anything and said in desperation, "What can be done?"'

He was not a quitter. He had a long track record of ingenious ploys. On a previous assignment which involved crawling around in mud he had been refused permission by the BBC to spend £6 on dungarees. They told him to use either his own cash or old clothes. A month later they failed to notice that a £6 expenses claim from de Jaeger was for 'entertaining press officer, Mr Dungarees'. And as he and the Swiss Tourist Office rep combed Lugano, he remembered a lakeside hotel in nearby Castiglione (a lovely name for a spaghetti-growing town) where he had once stayed.

It had laurel trees with leaves on all the year round, tall trees. So I said, 'We'll do it here. Let's go down into Lugano and get some handmade spaghetti.' We did that, put the strands of spaghetti in a big wooden platter, took that in the car and drove back. But by the time we got there, the damn things wouldn't hang up. They'd dried out. So we cooked them, tried to put them on the trees, and this time they fell off because they were so slippery.

Then this tourist guy had a brilliant idea – put the spaghetti between damp cloths. That worked and we got local girls to hang them up – about ten pounds' worth. Then we got the girls into national costume and filmed them climbing on ladders with these baskets, filling them up, and laying them out in the sun. And we said in the script, with a guitar playing in the background, 'We have this marvellous festival. The first harvest of the spaghetti.'

He rewarded his amateur actors with a spaghetti feast, and filmed that too.

Back in London, with four days to go before transmission, Wheeler viewed the clips and was delighted. The hotel was outstandingly pretty, he recalled later, the girls full of vim, and small details like the ageing wicker harvest baskets added to the realistic air. 'The pictures were convincing and now I tried to make it equally convincing in the script.' As Peacock says, he triumphed. Wheeler clattered out on his typewriter:

It is not only in Britain that spring this year has taken everyone by surprise. Here in the Ticino, on the borders of Switzerland and Italy, the slopes overlooking Lake Lugano have already burst into flower at least a fortnight earlier than usual. But what, you may ask, has the early and welcome arrival of bees and blossom to do with food? Well it is simply that the past winter, one of the mildest in living memory, has had its effect in other ways as well. Most important of all, it's resulted in an exceptionally heavy spaghetti crop. The last two weeks of March are an anxious time for the spaghetti farmer. There is always the chance of a late frost which, while not entirely ruining the crop, generally impairs the flavour and makes it difficult for him to obtain top prices in world markets. But now these dangers are over and the spaghetti harvest goes forward.

Spaghetti cultivation here in Switzerland is not, of course, carried out on anything like the tremendous scale of the Italian industry. Many of you, I am sure, will have seen pictures of vast spaghetti plantations in the Po Valley. For the Swiss, however, it tends to be more of a family affair. Another reason why this may be a bumper year lies in the virtual disappearance of the spaghetti weevil, the tiny creature whose depredations have caused much concern in the past. After picking, the spaghetti is laid out to dry in the warm Alpine air. Many people are very puzzled by the fact that spaghetti is produced in such uniform lengths. This is the result of many years of patient endeavour by plant breeders who have succeeded in producing the perfect spaghetti. Now the harvest is marked by a traditional meal. Toasts to the new crop are drunk in these boccalinos [pitchers, duly filmed by de Jaeger], then the waiters enter bearing the ceremonial dish. This is of course spaghetti – picked early in the day, dried in the sun, and so brought fresh from garden to table at the very peak of condition. For those who love this dish, there is nothing like real home-grown spaghetti.

It was a masterly 350 words, suited to the sonorous cadences of Dimbleby who saw the script and fortunately agreed to join the prank with his own dignified version of glee. The references to weevils and boccalinos lent authenticity, in the same way as the wicker baskets had in the filming, and touches such as 'Many of you, I am sure, will have seen pictures of vast spaghetti plantations in the Po Valley' were pure *Panorama*, pure Dimbleby. We must have seen them, countless viewers decided, lured by the 'Many of you' and lulled by the 'I am sure'. The explanation of uniform length, as found in packet spaghetti, was another excellent touch.

The film ran for three minutes and was dubbed with Wheeler's commentary, read by Dimbleby, and given the romantic backing of 'A Neapolitan Love Song' by the composer Walter Stott and 'Spring in Ravenna' by Hans May. Peacock and the duty director Catherine Dove, one of the few women working for *Panorama* in this very male era, drew up the running order and put spaghetti last, after a wine-tasting battle between Gaston Berlemont, the landlord of Soho's 'French pub', the York Minster in Greek Street, and a City wine merchant called Thomas Layton. Because of the oppressive nature of the BBC hierarchy at the time, which was sensitive to political and public criticism to a degree unimaginable today, Peacock kept controversial cards close to his chest and the pre-transmission publicity handouts mentioned only another item, an outside broadcast of the Duke of Edinburgh attending the premiere of the war film *The Yangtse Incident*. The other main clip in the programme was a debate between Malcolm Muggeridge, also a *Panorama* reporter at the time, and two MPs about the recent release from jail of Archbishop Makarios, the rebellious leader of Greek Cypriots, which had prompted Lord Salisbury to resign from Harold Macmillan's government. It was all a perfect context for the pasta ambush.

Peacock and the team had some reason to be nervous, however. The Electrical Trades Union was taking unpredictable industrial action at the time over the manning of a new lighting control system at the BBC's Riverside Studios. An emergency script was drafted for Dimbleby in case the pictures went down. Any such disruptive flak would be taken, the programme makers hoped, by *Hancock's Half Hour* which went out earlier in the evening. But *Panorama*'s technical staff were warned to be ready for a delayed start to their slot.

Ensuring that every last strand of the bountiful spaghetti harvest is fully gathered in. *BBC*

It wasn't needed. All went well. Dimbleby moved in his stately way round the set, with its 24 separate props delivered earlier in the day to Lime Grove – among them 25 bound copies of *Punch* magazine, three potted ferns and six armchairs. He introduced Muggeridge & Co., segued to the outside broadcast in Leicester Square and moved calmly on to a special report from one of *Panorama*'s star reporters, the former runner and future MP Chris Chataway, in Poland. The wine-bibbers then appeared, purring and debating over bottles which they were tasting blind – Beaujolais 1955, Châteauneuf-du-Pape 1955, Corton 1946, Château Calon-Ségur 1952, Château La Mission Haut-Brion 1950 and Château La Lagune 1950. And then Dimbleby went deadpan into 'And finally . . .' mode. 'And now from wine to food,' he said, straight to camera in his engaging and entirely trustworthy style. 'We end *Panorama* tonight with a special report from the Swiss Alps.'

Cue the marvellous film, the brilliant commentary, the swelling music. The millions watched as yet another fascinating 'window on the world' (*Panorama*'s catchphrase) was opened for their information, education and entertainment. Then Dimbleby reappeared and gave them a whopper of a nudge that all was not what it seemed. 'Now we say goodnight,' he signed off, 'on this *first day of April*.'

Most of the millions watching missed his clue. De Jaeger's long-contemplated spoof had scored an extraordinary bull's-eye. Among those tuned in was the BBC's director-general, Sir Ian Jacob, a former army general who tried to keep a close eye on *Panorama*. He knew that its Young Turk editor – Peacock was only 27 – and his stars such as Chataway (known on air as 'the chap who never takes no for an answer') liked to feel they were breaking new ground. There had been a huge row in 1956 when Brendan Behan was interviewed by Malcolm Muggeridge and used the F-word for the first time on British TV. Luckily he was so drunk that hardly any viewers noticed, but the programme's producer only kept his job by describing vividly to a disciplinary hearing how he had poured all the remaining drink in the Green Room down a sink to prevent the Irish playwright from collapsing completely. As recently as February, when *Panorama* had broadcast the first birth of a baby to be shown on TV, Jacob had sent in a team to make sure that the film was edited to show nothing more than the infant's head. Even so, the corporation was attacked by the *Daily Sketch* after transmission for showing the 'worst taste ever'.

The spaghetti caper was not a political exposé or (as it seemed at the time) a broadcasting milestone to die for, so as the day of the broadcast approached Peacock had relaxed his caginess about giving senior colleagues notice of his plans. His immediate superior Leonard Miall, the Head of Television Talks, knew what was going on. He sent a precautionary message at the last minute to Sir Ian Jacob's office alerting him to the fact that there was going to be an April Fool.

As seems to happen through Sod's Law in such cases, someone failed to pass it on. The next day Jacob and Miall met in a corridor at Lime Grove television centre and the DG promptly started on about spaghetti. Miall's heart must have missed a beat, but Jacob was all warmth and academic curiosity. He said: 'When I saw that item, I said to my wife, "I don't think spaghetti grows on trees," so we looked it up in *Encyclopædia Britannica*. Do you know, Miall, *Encyclopædia Britannica* doesn't even mention spaghetti.'

The director-general had summarised the genius of this April Fool. De Jaeger and Wheeler had given a textbook lesson in choosing an ideal subject for the time, as well as handling it with aplomb and a first-class team. The Victorians and Edwardians might have laughed at Herbert Campbell's spaghetti jokes, but the dish was still very much a post-war novelty on English tables in the 1950s. For most people it was the only 'foreign' food cooked at home apart from 'British Army curry', that strange concoction of curry powder, raisins, crisps and baked beans brought back from India. Soldiers had enjoyed pasta in wartime Italy and many Italian prisoners of war in Britain had stayed and helped to popularise it here. Spaghetti was also the stuff of fun, rather than serious inquiry about where it came from and how it was made.

And so the nation, and later much of the British Commonwealth and the United States where the film was re-shown within days, was seriously fooled. Memories posted on websites describe how families sat rapt. 'We knew nothing about spaghetti in Yorkshire,' says one. 'It only ever came in a tin,' says another. In Manchester, a Swiss student was rushed into the front room by her host family to watch. In Bristol, two boys protested angrily that they knew spaghetti was mined. Within minutes of Dimbleby's sign-off, calls started to flood in to the BBC, some raising doubts but many more asking where they could buy spaghetti plants in Britain. Miall, who had entered thoroughly into the spirit of things, went to the phone exchange in Lime Grove to listen in. The calls came in incessantly for the next two hours, he recalled. 'Some were from viewers who had enjoyed the joke – including one from Bristol who complained that spaghetti didn't grow vertically, it grew horizontally. But mainly the calls were requests for the BBC to settle family arguments: the husband knew it must be true that spaghetti grew on a bush because Richard Dimbleby had said so and the wife knew it was made with flour and water, but neither could convince the other.'

Before the end of transmissions, which in those days finished around midnight with a small white dot and a loud continuous sound to rouse any viewer who had fallen asleep, the corporation broadcast a grave statement.

The BBC has received a mixed reaction to a spoof documentary broadcast this evening about spaghetti crops in Switzerland. The hoax *Panorama* programme, narrated by distinguished broadcaster Richard Dimbleby, featured a family from Ticino in Switzerland carrying out their annual spaghetti harvest. It showed women carefully plucking strands of spaghetti from a tree and laying them in the sun to dry. But some viewers failed to see the funny side of the broadcast and criticised the BBC for airing the item on what is supposed to be a serious factual programme. Others, however, were so intrigued they wanted to find out where they could purchase their very own spaghetti bush.

Spaghetti is not a widely-eaten food in the UK and is considered by many as an exotic delicacy. Mr Dimbleby explained how each year the end of March is a very anxious time for spaghetti harvesters all over Europe as severe frost can impair the flavour of the spaghetti. He also explained how each strand of spaghetti always grows to the same length thanks to years of hard work by generations of growers. This is believed to be one of the first times the medium of television has been used to stage an April Fool's Day hoax.

Not everyone was pleased. The *Daily Telegraph* carried the censorious headline next morning: 'BBC fools about with spaghetti', and a significant number of calls and letters lamented a betrayal of trust. A grammar school teacher was typical. She described how she had always encouraged pupils to watch Mr Dimbleby. She felt let down. She had a point too. The following year the film was shown at a school in Chicago as a piece of genuine reportage. Others contacted the *Telegraph* to condemn the whole affair as 'childish and irresponsible'. Purists among them ruled its 9 p.m. transmission out of order because 'April Fool's jokes ought to stop at noon in accordance with tradition'.

The BBC did its best to reassure such critics – it would be a long time before April Fool's fell on a Monday again, said officials. They meanwhile took a playful line in following up the hoax. After a few days, anyone who rang or wrote in about growing their own spaghetti was advised: place a sprig of spaghetti in a tin of tomato sauce and hope for the best.

Internally, all was joy. *Panorama* staff scurried around doing things like sending a film to the US network NBC which rang overnight asking for a copy. The director of outside broadcasts S.J. de Lotbinière, whose own rich experience included a series transmitted from haunted houses with special ghost-recording equipment, told Peacock: 'I travelled this morning in a BBC van with a fair cross section of BBC staff. They were all delighted with *Panorama*'s spaghetti item – as was I.' The ultra-cautious Jacob, once satisfied that there wasn't going to be a row, sent a note with a suggestion which was daring for him: that the BBC's house magazine *Ariel* should carry a piece preserving some of de Jaeger's stills and Wheeler's commentary for posterity. On 5 April Miall passed this news on to both men. His herogram to Wheeler, preserved at Caversham on flimsy copy paper, reads: 'The commentary you wrote for the spaghetti harvest item was brilliant. Many congratulations.' To de Jaeger he said: 'The spaghetti harvest was a splendid idea, beautifully shot and organised. This item has caused a great deal of delight one way and another. Thank you very much indeed.' Executives were more cautious with their superlatives in those days than they are now and this was praise indeed.

But it was outdone, as the days went by, by the general public. The

BBC archive has a clutch of original telegrams to Dimbleby – the man in charge of the programme as far as viewers were concerned – and a typed-out sheet of other messages taken down by the staff answering the phones. At the bottom of this is a heartfelt message in blue ink, almost certainly from someone who had been trying to cope with days of requests about where to buy spaghetti plants. 'Well done *Panorama*,' it says. 'The above may amuse you. Thank God there are still some people who can see a joke.'

The tongue-in-cheek responders included the Bodycombe family of Swansea who cabled 'Can fix fly', meaning the weevil, and Mr Booth from Claverly in Birmingham whose telegram said: 'What nonsense. Everyone knows spaghetti is a root crop grown in radio holes drilled to length by trained worms.' From Margate, an unlikely-sounding Fred Farina (the Italian for flour) criticised the 'unsporting' Swiss for picking spaghetti out of season and the Kidstons of Andover requested *Panorama* to come and see their fishcake bulbs. Two viewers launched into verse, a traditional response to media funny items. Mr Devas of Retford was pithy: 'Spaghetti that grows/As everyone knows/Doesn't taste/Like paste.' Norman Fieldhouse in Birmingham was more lyrical: 'Oh tell us where spaghetti bred/Or in the bush or baker's shed/How begot how nourished/Not as *Panorama* said.'

Very wisely, *Panorama* rested on its laurels. There were no more Dimbleby spoofs. Even at the height of the post-broadcast fun, the programme's office wrote to an excited film company in Glasgow rejecting a proposed sequel. It would be 'very much of an anti-climax to spend any more time talking about past'asciutta', the letter said, adding insincerely: 'Perhaps next April.' The Current Affairs flagship needed to sail on, as did her crew. De Jaeger continued to work as a sought-after cameraman and wrote a fascinating book about one of the stories he covered – Hitler's unrealised plan for a European art gallery in his native Linz, stuffed with treasures looted from all over the continent. Everyone else involved went on to illustrious careers, although Michael Peacock must have wondered if some ghost with spaghetti connections was hoaxing him when BBC2 opened in 1964 in April (albeit not on the first) with him as controller. Battersea Power Station went up in flames and a huge power cut silenced the start of the opening night's transmissions from a Television Centre lit only by candles.

The spaghetti film meanwhile lived on and still does. You can watch it on your computer via the BBC's website. It has often been rebroadcast, and continues to be, and although the world's knowledge of spaghetti has grown exponentially since 1957, some viewers are gulled every time. Although a chain of pasta houses in the United States used huge stills from the prank as decoration, and although an American spaghetti firm copied the harvest idea in an obviously unrealistic TV advertisement, the skills of de Jaeger, Wheeler and Dimbleby have remained potent. Jack Paar, a leading US talk show host, showed the film deadpan in the 1960s and had hundreds of calls asking why his studio audience had laughed at it. His successor Johnny Carson was berated for supposedly mocking simple, poverty-stricken pasta farmers when he showed the film on network TV and chortled along, without explaining why.

And if *Panorama* knew about quitting when you are ahead, that did not stop a rich succession of later broadcast hoaxes. You could call them . . .

CHARLES DE JAEGER'S CHILDREN . . .

FUN DOWN UNDER

The spaghetti harvest soon prompted direct copies, with the Australian Broadcasting Company in the van. Much taken by *Panorama*'s weevil, the Aussies focused on the devastation of the crop in their own country by the 'spaghetti worm'. Like the Colorado beetle and similar pests, this was an insatiable eater. It attacked the unripe spaghetti from the inside, cruelly leaving much of the husk which was then worthless. Pesticides couldn't be used to destroy it because they made the spaghetti unfit to be eaten. The programme lived up to de Jaeger and Wheeler's high standards, with footage of infested bushes being burned and haggard farmers giving interviews about facing financial ruin. An appeal for donations to help them had thousands of good-hearted suckers going to banks across the country the next day. The following week, ABC broadcast an item about how the hoax was made, which proved one step too far. Grumps created such a fuss about wasting government money that TV April Fool's jokes dropped for years.

STOCKING SCIENCE

Why did thousands of Swedes march over to their TV sets with nylon stockings on April Fool's Day 1962 and stretch them over the screen? They had been told to do so by the monopoly TV company's technical expert, Kjell Stensson, a convincingly serious character, who was interviewed about a technological breakthrough. Sweden at the time had only black-and-white TV but Stensson explained that new transmission systems meant that covering the screen with nylon would produce colour. He then demonstrated this – an easy thing to do on black-and-white TV where the result on his set had to be taken on trust. A very large proportion of Sweden's seven million population admitted carrying out the test. In vain. They had to wait for real colour, and the joy of watching snooker on TV at last, until 1970. It was introduced, nostalgically, on April Fool's Day that year.

JUMP FOR JOY

No one who has seen him on TV or heard him on air will ever forget Patrick Moore, who was an ideal presenter to carry off an astronomical hoax. As weighty as Richard Dimbleby, with an added air of batty enthusiasm which only added to his credibility, he announced early on April Fool's Day 1976 that a 'unique astronomical event' was going to occur at 9.47 a.m. As the little planet Pluto passed behind Jupiter, he said, a 'gravitational alignment' would reduce the Earth's gravity for a few moments. Anyone who jumped into the air at 9.47 would experience a strange floating sensation. They did too, or at least hundreds of them thought they did. The BBC was flooded with appreciative calls from people claiming to have floated, including a woman who said that she and eleven friends had been wafted from their chairs and orbited gently around the room.

HONEY TRAP

In mid-March 1950 the New Zealand Broadcasting Service issued the first copy of an annual memo to the country's radio stations, reminding would-be April Foolers that NZ broadcasting is dedicated to telling the truth. The man responsible for this was called Phil Shone, a DJ on a station called 1ZB, who on April Fool's Day 1949 played a blinder about wasps. A mile-wide swarm was heading towards Auckland, he said, and householders should take a number of steps to avoid multiple stings. These included leaving honey-smeared jam-jar traps outside their houses and going out only with socks rolled up over trousers (wasps apparently spot a bare ankle from far away). Hundreds complied until Phil came clean later in the morning. The director of the NZBS, Professor James Shelley, was not amused. The solemn memo the following year came from him.

CUTTING THE ONION

On April Fool's Day 1965 BBC TV introduced a professor who had invented 'smellovision'. He conducted a demonstration of the new technique, which transmitted smells from the studio to viewers at home. Coffee was brewed and onions cut – but the resulting tears were of laughter at Broadcasting House as people phoned in to say how effective the method was. The power of suggestion. But the BBC was lucky to get away with this one. A full six years earlier, a pioneering technique called Aroma-Rama had fed scents through a theatre's air conditioning to accompany a film called *Behind the Great Wall*. In 1960 Mike Todd Jr. used a process actually called Smell-o-Vision to waft scents to the audience during his *A Scent of Mystery*. The system got out of sync and failed to account for smells lingering after their subject had vanished from the screen. Nevertheless, another American film director, John Waters, tried again in 1982. His Odorama method gave filmgoers scent scratchcards to use at appropriate moments. It proved too much of a fag to catch on.

THE MICE THAT ROARED

Strange and wonderful animals have always been central to April Fool's, but when they are discovered by David Attenborough you buy it. Another Dimbleby in his own field of natural history, the distinguished broadcaster introduced Radio 3 listeners in 1975 to a previously unknown species of night-singing tree mice. Known as *Mus endrophilus*, the dear little creatures came from the Pacific Sheba Islands and they actually sang for the station's listeners, who mostly tune in for very high-quality classical music. Attenborough elaborated that local people on the Shebas used the webbed feet of the mice as reeds in their own musical instruments and there was more soundtrack of these. There was much disappointment, tinged with admiration for the straight-faced spoof, when the truth became known.

OOH-LA-LA

Radio 3 was generally a bit mischievous in the 1970s and in 1972 it decided to test its listeners' French on April Fool's Day. How many knew that the word *mensonge* meant 'lie'? Those that did may have recognised that an author discussed in the programme *In Parenthesis* called Henri Mensonge was possibly dodgy, especially as his book was called *La Fornication Comme Une Acte Culturelle*. The merits or otherwise of this treatise on sexual intercourse as a cultural act were debated by a round table of eggheads, who delved deeply into its alleged theory that early-Seventies Europe was living 'in an age of metaphysical rape'. The discussion then moved on to consider the question 'Is *Is* Is?' before the playing of incomprehensible music. There was very little reaction.

BEWARE OF THE TREES

Dutch elm disease was no joke as it effectively wiped out the species in Britain, but Spike Milligan could get away with anything. In 1973 he appeared on TV as an elderly Dr Clothier who claimed that a colleague called Dr Emily Lang from the London School of Pathological and Environmental Medicine had discovered that the disease could be transmitted to people. It went for redheads in particular, because their bloodcount was similar to soil conditions surrounding the roots of affected trees. If infected, their hair would turn yellow and then fall out, so they should keep away from woodland. Spike Milligan was hard to disguise and the number of dupes is thought to have been small. But these were prophetic notions of cross-species transmission, later horribly realised with bovine spongiform encephalopathy. The London School of Pathological and Environmental Medicine, grand though it sounds, does not exist.

POSTMAN'S KNOCK

Genial and with excellent moustaches, Tom Jackson was one of the few big union leaders who was held in some affection by the British public. So his presence on screen helped to lull viewers into believing the BBC's 1977 April Fool – a proposal to alter postal addresses to the German system which puts the house number after the name of the street. Jackson rumbled out a convincing protest on behalf of his Union of Post Office Workers, whose members would have to be expensively retrained. Large numbers of viewers, still sore about having to remember postcodes, backed his stand and the reform has never been introduced. Not that it was ever going to be anyway.

TIME MOVES ON . . .

An extremely ingenious April Fool in 1980 saw the BBC announce that Big Ben was to be brought up to date by replacing its venerable faces with digital screens. This was exactly what was happening on millions of British wrists at the time. The choice of a famous icon and a topic at the back of people's minds was truly in the spaghetti tradition. The corporation's Japanese service gilded the lily by announcing that the redundant metal hands of the clock were for sale. Among an immediate spate of offers was one from a Japanese seaman who had tuned in while crossing the Atlantic Ocean. Big Ben remains inviolate although it has recently had trouble with the reliability of its famous 'Bong!' chimes.

. . . AND SO DO THE DAYS

This is an old one, with all sorts of variants based on the supposed ability to 'save daylight' by getting up at different times. Hoaxes at home often involve a quick spin of the clock's hands forwards or backwards, or changing the date on desk calendars. In spite of all that, plenty of people believed Capital Radio in London in 1979 when they announced that the British calendar needed to be 're-synchronised' (a good April Fool word) with the rest of the world. Because so much time had been gained by annual switches to and from British Summer Time, a whole two days had to be lost, according to the news item. The government had chosen to sacrifice 5 and 12 April. Genuinely anxious enquiries included an employer who wanted to know if she still had to pay her staff for the lost days; and a woman who wondered what to do about her birthday, which fell on 5 April.

ODE TO JOY

Stout denials that the heir to the throne was caught out by this one, but rumours persist that Prince Charles got in touch with the *Today* programme on Radio 4. The reason was an item on April Fool's Day 1999 announcing that 'God Save the Queen' was to be replaced by the European 'anthem', the *Ode to Joy* from Beethoven's Ninth Symphony, which was then sung lustily by a group of pupils from the German school in London. It hasn't happened but the joke encouraged discussion of more up-to-date alternatives to the dreary old song. Australia meanwhile went ahead with a replacement but sadly turned down 'Waltzing Matilda' in favour of something called 'Advance Australia Fair'.

PRACTICAL JOKES

If media April Fool's hoaxes have a fault, it's that they can get too complicated. Joe Public tends to stick to the simple – but often very effective – wheeze when he or she stages a prank outside their own home.

ZEBRA IN THE NIGHT

Road safety is a serious issue, so I must say at once that this should not be repeated, just enjoyed as a historical one-off. Somehow, pranksters found a time overnight on 31 March 2000 when the M3 motorway through Hampshire was quiet to paint all six lanes with a zebra crossing. The size of the area daubed with white stripes meant that quite a little team must have been assembled, possibly to make a point about the motorway cutting off neighbouring communities in the Farnborough area. They thoughtfully used emulsion which motorway maintenance staff sprayed off in time to avoid the misery of rush-hour disruption and there were no public complaints.

CLOSED FOR THE DAY

Cutting off and closing down communities is a long-standing tabloid prank, or one which April Foolers use in the hope of getting newspaper headlines. In 1981 persons unknown went to elaborate lengths to put notices saying 'Closed' at every entry point into Romsey Abbey, Hampshire, overnight on 31 March. Diversion signs were erected and official-looking press releases from the county council arrived in the morning post on local media newsdesks. In 1986 DJs in Providence, Rhode Island, broadcast public service announcements that the city was closed because of unspecified industrial action. They gave out a contact number which actually belonged to the rival local radio station. Both stunts were children of the more ambitious pranksters who organised road signs saying 'Island full – sorry' in 1978 on the road to Anglesey, or Ynys Mon. The notices were highly professional, albeit not bilingual as they would be today, and many motorists did indeed turn back. The story was treated as genuine by the BBC, ITN and Liverpool's Radio City until Gwynedd police got their act together. It was given added legs by the fact that on the other side of the country the Lincolnshire resort of Mablethorpe became so overcrowded that the tourist office actually did ask police to turn late arrivals away.

ON THE ROCKS

This one's a bit more complex and a lot more expensive. In the days before fridges, wealthy people used to buy enormous hunks of ice from traders who cut the stuff from Scottish mountain-tops or glaciers in the Alps. So the Australian food company millionaire Dick Smith seemed to be on safe ground when he announced a scheme for towing icebergs to Sydney Harbour where they would be cut into neat cubes for sale at ten cents each. The ice would actually improve the flavour of drinks, he claimed, as it came from one of the last pure and unpolluted wildernesses of the world. Needless to say, the first berg arrived on April the first, to a welcome from large crowds after advance publicity in local newspapers and on radio and TV. The truth emerged when it started to rain and a mixture of fire-fighting foam and shaving cream slid in damp globs from the iceberg's plastic-sheeted timber frame.

5

Islands in the Sun

The Paradise of Fools, to few unknown
JOHN MILTON, *PARADISE LOST*, BOOK III

*t*WENTY YEARS AFTER *PANORAMA*'S SPAGHETTI CAME THE
MOST SUCCESSFUL APRIL FOOL IN NEWSPAPER HISTORY. It
had its unlikely origins in the humble 'Special Reports' section
of the *Guardian*, responsible for pull-out advertising supplements
which combined editorial material with related adverts and used to fill
the nation's litterbins the following day. They still flutter out
occasionally, but both advertisers and newspapers are much more
sophisticated than in the 1970s, the genre's heyday. Even then, special
reports were one of the world's great examples of wasted effort;
millions of words which hardly anyone read.

They made money, otherwise they would never have existed, even
if the eccentric range of bodies which commissioned them had more
than their share of bad payers. But journalists and advertising
executives mostly shuddered at the mention of the phrase 'special
reports' and hoped that the choice of writer or advert-hunter would
fall elsewhere. The only compensation was extra pay for the chore
and, sometimes, an exhilaration when the most unlikely subject – say
a comprehensive look at electric lighting flex – turned out to be
strangely fascinating. Unlike the overcrowded main paper, a special
report had unbelievable amounts for space for its writers to go on and
on.

Soon after I moved from London to Leeds for the *Guardian*, I was grateful that Special Reports decided to do a big number on the Yorkshire and the Humber region. It was down to me, and I learned enough to make me an expert for years on the local economy, arts, sport and everything else. Likewise, in my earlier life on the *Bath Evening Chronicle*, I had to write six pages for a special report on a single city-centre road, Green Street. Every shop, business and especially pub (the Green Tree has remained a lifelong favourite) had a story to tell. I could have written a book.

So it was at the *Guardian* in the 1970s. Along with *The Times* and the *Financial Times*, the paper found that a monthly focus on a recondite subject brought in lots of money from themed advertisements. The subjects were impressively varied, from sleep via shaving cream to Whither Nigeria?, and the man in charge of thinking them up was no dud. He was an advertising rep called Philip Davies who was a born wheeler-dealer and a man with his finger on the popular pulse.

Davies was the son of a printing machine minder on the *Surrey Mirror*. Newspapers were in his blood and before the *Guardian* he worked on his family's local, the *Woking News and Mail*, and then on bigger papers in Surrey and Hampshire. But he was also a natural entrepreneur and by the time he joined the *Guardian* in 1974, he was wealthy enough to spend a hefty slice of his £3,000 salary on a first-class season ticket from Farnham. This gave him the chance to make interesting contacts and led to extra-curricular coups which were legendary and a source of some friction with senior colleagues. 'I don't know what became of him but I'm sure he's very, very rich,' says the managing director at the time, Gerry Taylor. 'He was forever doing things he shouldn't have done in our time. If I recollect rightly, he once bought up all the seats at the Oval cricket ground, when it was modernised, and sold them to Surrey fans.'

Davies was forever coming up with bright, money-making ideas. He suggested an instant Guardian book on Elvis Presley, for instance, putting the case for overnight action to a senior manager at the *Guardian* on the day that The King died. Davies got only a withering look and the snooty response: 'Eff off Philip, this is the *Guardian* . . .' Unchastened, he enlisted a star reporter and a sub-editor and went ahead, repeating the exercise on the deaths of Bing Crosby and Pope Paul VI. The papal biography ended the series, alas, as the new pontiff John Paul I died in his turn after only 33 days in office and few people wanted to read about his predecessor any more.

Davies had many other scrapes and adventures, including complex advertising negotiations with an African dictator which were to be significant in his April Fool. The fun was one of the reasons why a natural entrepreneur who is now a very wealthy man, as Gerry Taylor foretold, put up with the dogsbody Special Reports job and its measly £3,000 a year. He also loved the excitement and the deadlines, and felt himself to be a 'Guardian man'. His father had taken the paper all his life. In Special Reports he found his own little state-within-a-state. 'He was very bright but narrow,' recalls Gerry Taylor with the reluctant admiration of someone who still wonders what Davies was doing half the time. 'Special Reports was considered a lowly job in the ads department but he seized it and made it work. He reminds me of Peter Stringfellow' (the 1980s club-owner from Yorkshire who mesmerised London by turning drossy ventures into gold dust). Another colleague, after I told him of Davies's unusual range of interests, murmured, 'Ah, the Barnum of Farnham.' In terms of imagination and enthusiasm, it was a phrase well coined.

Davies's independence armoured him against sneers from lofty colleagues like the Elvis manager or journalists who mistrusted any close links between editorial and the business of earning revenue. Ignoring his many successes, which they didn't read but which carried incredible amounts of accurate information about the haulage trade or the tercentenary of Anglo-Dutch bilateral treaties, they mocked the occasional helping of rubbish, such as the unreadable pages bought by North Korea and filled with the turgid opinions of that country's dictator Kim Il-sung. Davies still recalls how the paper dropped a Special Report on men's magazines. It had taken weeks of hard work but the high command, who also barred adverts for women's underwear and loft ladders, didn't consider it the Guardian's type of thing.

But it was Davies who in the end may have a wider and more lasting fame than any of the journalist lions. For the Guardian's great hoax, the invention of an entire country called San Serriffe, was his idea. 'The *Financial Times* was always doing special reports on little countries I'd never heard of,' he says. 'I was thinking about April Fool's Day 1977 and I thought: why don't we just make a country up?' He put the notion to Gerry Taylor and in turn the witty editor at the time Peter Preston, who were both intrigued. Crucial enthusiasm, though, came from the second-in-command on the editorial side of Special Reports, Stuart St Clair Legge. He was the man who suggested the title which was to become a legend. San Serriffe – part typographic pun, part credible name for a tropical isle. It also had the special appropriateness for the *Guardian* of challenging spelling. During its long relationship with San Serriffe, starting with the original supplement itself, the paper has printed the name with carefree inconsistency using every possible variation of 'r's and 'f's and on one occasion two 'e's.

Davies's original outline was modest. He had once wondered about doing a one-page special with backing by Heineken, or a similarly jokey advertiser, on brewing in an invented country. His new idea initially involved a page or maybe two at the back of the paper. The report would gently mimic the usual thorough examinations of higher education in, say, Botswana, or the prospects for tourism on the Ivory Coast. A nice little joke, like the April Fool spoof he had done a few years earlier for a shoe shop advertisement in the *Surrey and Hants News*. They got lots of applications for a job walking Hush Puppies before opening and after 5 p.m.

There were risks, however. Only five years earlier the respected travel correspondent of *The Times* John Carter had lost his job over an April Fool involving distant lands. In 1972, on a hugely busy news day which saw direct rule introduced into the bloody chaos of Northern Ireland, the paper ran a special feature in its Saturday Review to mark the centenary of the travel agency Thomas Cook. In a wicked moment, Carter typed out an addition to the copy which offered 1,000 places on a special centenary tour of the world 'at 1872 prices'. An extraordinary itinerary via Cape Kennedy space centre, the Great Barrier Reef, Mount Fuji, the Taj Mahal, the Valley of the Kings and at least a dozen major capitals appeared to be available to prompt applicants for a bargain £220.50.

Friday April 1 1977 17

SAN SERRIFFE

a Guardian special report

THE TEN YEARS of independence which San Serriffe celebrates today have been a period of economic expansion and social development probably unrivalled by any other new nation. With this achievement has gone a determined attempt, in part successful, to maintain the outward forms of a parliamentary democracy. This special report, edited and introduced by Geoffrey Taylor, attempts to recount the remarkable transformation in the life of the Republic, to inform British investors and traders of the opportunities which have been and are being created, and not least to encourage companies trading with the Republic to call attention to their share in its development. Rapid growth brings its own problems, not all of which can be solved in total composure. The survey allows some of those problems to be brought under closer scrutiny.

The President, General D.d. Pica

GUIDE TO THE REPUBLIC

Location: Northwest of the Seychelle Islands, Colombo 1,550 miles.

Area: 9,724 sq. m.

Population: 1975 census 1,782,789 consisting of Juppah I Europeans and minorities 640,000; Flongs 594,000; Creoles, 251,000; Malactones 117,000; Arabs 92,000; others 89,000.

Capital: Bodoni.

Tourist centres: Caramondo, Villa Pica, Gillcamesi, Cap Em, Limbo.

Climate: Oceanic equatorial. Rains mainly May-October and early January.

Currency: The San Serriffe Corona (100 ants) has become one of the hardest currencies, standing at 0.1 = £4.50.

Transit: San Serriffe Airways from Gatwick or via Mogadishu.

Health: Smallpox, cholera, typhus, and lassa fever vaccinations required.

Customs: No Customs duties are levied on tourists or commercial properties.

Language: English is the working language. Colon is used on ceremonial occasions, and there is a language (K. Flongs) indigenous to the Flongs.

Three point key to prosperity

LANDMARKS IN HISTORY

1431

1432-39

1875

1929-35

April 1 1967

June 1967

August 1969

May 12 1975

Geoffrey Taylor

Readers should have noticed the date and the tell-tale name of the contact for their letters and phone calls: Miss Avril Foley. But hundreds rang *The Times* asking to speak to her and almost 3,000 sent letters requesting a place. The rather pompous crew who ran the 'top people's paper' were aghast. The editor William Rees-Mogg was having tea at his Somerset mansion with his managing director Marmaduke Hussey when the Press Association rang and let them in on the hoax. Carter was dismissed and the assistant features editor Margaret Allen had a narrow escape; after debate, her offer to resign was turned down. It was all an almighty cock-up, Carter insisted (and he was later reinstated). The spoof had been a private office joke and was clipped to a note saying 'NOT for the news pages' with a battery of exclamation marks. As happens in such cases, the note apparently became detached and the copy was marked, subbed and revised by a succession of colleagues who were blind to Avril and the fantastic nature of the world tour. Was the *Guardian* really going to go down the same path?

Yes. The crucial difference from *The Times* debacle was that San Serriffe was no back-of-an-envelope wheeze but a highly sophisticated vehicle for mounds of advertising revenue. There might be some angry and made-to-feel-foolish readers, but the panache of the deception would keep their numbers small. Ironically, the *Guardian*'s relatively new managing director Gerry Taylor was an enemy of special reports because he thought they diverted energy from ordinary ads in the main paper. He still recalls with a shudder how, soon after he joined, the *Guardian* published an issue with only one display advertisement in the entire edition. He was also from an advertising agency background and like all Londoners, had seen the rubbish bins overflowing with chucked-away supplements. The paper might be getting revenue from them, but advertisers were not getting their money's worth. That stuck in his teeth.

Phil Davies's inspiration was another matter. Taylor's sense of fun and imagination leapt at the possibilities of the entirely fake island. Advertisers would love it, he said. Like children, they could play along with bizarre riffs on the theme, building their own fantasies on an entirely false portfolio of San Serriffian geography and history which the *Guardian* would supply to them. So it proved. Philip Davies rang J. Walter Thompson, much the biggest advertising agency at the time, and asked to see the chief exec, Jeremy Bullmore. 'I didn't know him from Adam,' he said. 'But he was entranced. "Can we take on the whole thing?" he asked. "I'll deal with it myself."' It was almost unheard-of for this to happen with a special report, which was normally touted round every possible, bored agency on the books. Not with San Serriffe.

Sworn to secrecy, Bullmore called up his major clients and they queued to join in. Meanwhile another Taylor was deployed by Preston to oversee the editorial content. Phil Davies's cautious plans had been expanded into a full seven broadsheet pages – bigger than the entire paper had been within staff memory since the Second World War, and the biggest special report the *Guardian* had seen. It needed a star writer and editor to make sure that it was a tour de force.

Geoffrey Taylor was the man: a *Guardian* type to the marrow, a Northern lad who joined the paper in 1947 and rose rapidly and by his own bootstraps to become an expert on Africa. Long before San Serriffe, he was investigating palm-fringed shores and tropical savannahs. He interrupted his *Guardian* career to spend three happy years in the 1950s training local journalists in Nigeria. His colleagues in Manchester dispatched him there with presents of dark glasses, suntan oil and an army surplus solar topee. The air of Evelyn Waugh's novel *Scoop* surrounding the venture was reinforced by Taylor's quaint way of landing the job. He put an advertisement in *The Times* personal column asking for work in Africa. It was answered by one of that decade's equivalents of Waugh's Lord Copper: the press baron Cecil King whose empire included the *Lagos Daily Times*.

Taylor's talents included great skill at parody and a fondness for the curious and absurd in life. His father taught music at Sheffield City Grammar School, organised choirs and played the organ at the family's local church. His mother was also a musician and this joint inheritance tuned Geoffrey's ear. He never went to university, applying instead to the Royal Navy at the age of 17, but failed the medical and turned to the *Sheffield Telegraph* which took him on as a trainee. His background will have struck a chord when he applied for a job to A.P. Wadsworth, the editor of the *Guardian*, who most unusually for holders of that august post had left school himself at 15. Both men also shared an autodidact's enthusiasm for hoovering up knowledge, discovering strange and wonderful facts or names, and performing virtuoso solos with words.

Geoffrey was in the office when a special report on a dubious Middle Eastern state reached the paper complete with an agonised sub's note included by mistake in the finished text: 'Are we really sinking so low as to print this tendentious rubbish?' He knew the unctuous style and interminable detail of the supplements backwards, and set about realising San Serriffe with élan. He designed a shrunken semicolon-shaped version of New Zealand's twin islands, with which he had connections, and picking up Stuart Legge's theme, based everything on the rich vocabulary of print. Leading islanders such as the dictator General Pica and places like the capital Bodoni were named after fonts of type and their measurements. It seemed at times a high-risk strategy because some of the terms are well known even to laymen. Basic grammar, for instance, was commandeered; the word 'colon' had fortuitous echoes of 'colonists'. But the brio of the operation encouraged high-wire risks. Taylor and his band of fraudsters even got away with a wilderness area on the north island called Wodj of Type.

Some of the paper's best-known writers were enlisted in the scheme. One was Mark Arnold Foster, a distinguished foreign correspondent well known outside the paper for writing the epic TV series *The World at War*. Another was Tim Radford, a feature writer who first popularised the writings of Primo Levi in Britain and later became an award-winning science correspondent. As Geoffrey recalled later: 'Articles were commissioned, photographs distorted, charts drawn, history invented.' Like the Creation, albeit in rather more than seven days, an entire country took shape. Regularly supplied with top-secret drafts of the editorial copy, the advertisers joined in with a will. The islands were positioned off the Canaries and with just over three days to go, the final shape of the supplement was drawn up.

Then at six minutes past five in the late afternoon of 27 March two jumbo jets collided in fog at Tenerife airport, causing the worst

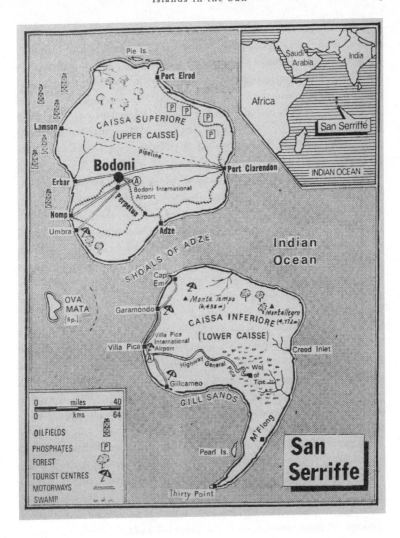

aviation disaster in the world, in which 583 people died. The delicate web of April Fool fantasy composed in Farringdon Road suddenly seemed marginal. Peter Preston teetered on the edge of pulling San Serriffe as had happened with the special report on men's magazines. But fortunately it was not abandoned. With a Herculean effort and overtime work at both the *Guardian* and the advertising agencies, the islands were relocated in the Indian Ocean. Their history, flora and fauna were completely revised and an inspirational article was added by the *Guardian's* science correspondent Anthony Tucker (known in the office as Phil and at his local pub in St Albans, where as night reporter I sometimes had to phone him, as Mick). Transferring the islands inspired the idea that San Serriffe should be a nation always on the move. As the sea relentlessly eroded its western coasts, Tucker explained, tides carried the material round and deposited it on bays in the east. As he and the paper's core Northern readers knew, this is a process which actually happens on the Yorkshire coast, where cliffs crumble into the sea and the debris is washed round Spurn Point by the tide, to resurface at Sunk Island and gradually enlarge the north bank of the Humber estuary.

So the evening of 31 March came, the presses rolled and San Serriffe indelibly joined the map of the world. Next morning, the phone calls started early, the letters followed later. Thousands of readers were taken in and when Geoffrey Taylor slipped into the office canteen in Farringdon Road in his usual unobtrusive way at lunchtime, the whole room burst into spontaneous applause. Spin-offs soon included 'I've been to San Serriffe' car stickers and a T-shirt from the islands which sold a record 12,000 to *Guardian* readers. Geoffrey was awarded a trophy called the Golden Leg by the TV comedians of *Monty Python's Flying Circus*. Modest to a fault, he handed it on to Davies who still has it on his mantelpiece in Devon, where his current entrepreneurial package includes a brewery next to Dartmoor prison which produces a beer called Jail Ale.

What did the world read that April Fool's Day – in a year, incidentally, when very few rivals came up with their own spoofs? BBC TV's *Nationwide* discovered a river in the North of England whose water made hair grow and the *Today* programme on Radio 4 ran a postal address spoof (see page 57). But apart from that, the joking was left to a clutch of BBC local radio stations whose quips were naturally parochial. Let Geoffrey introduce the islands that he and his colleagues conjured onto the map.

To those who have not followed its development at close hand, San Serriffe may be remembered only as a small archipelago, its main islands grouped roughly in the shape of a semi-colon, in the Indian Ocean. Until recently that would have been an adequate description: a punctuation mark, as it were, in a long chapter of oceanic exploration. But fifteen years ago came the phosphate industry, ten years ago the first tourist packages, and five years ago the resource which has added bounteously to its riches: oil.

San Serriffe's currency, the Corona, is linked to its oil, making it one of the hardest in the world. It seems to appreciate, to the concern of foreign bankers, with every barrel that flows down the pipeline from the west coast to Port Clarendon. The people, likewise, are linked to the life of island insouciance which they once enjoyed and from which the Government, under General M.J. Pica, is trying hard to advance them.

Although it is true that the resulting social tensions are evident even to the most transient visitor, he will also find a kindly and tolerant people; tolerant, in the eyes of people who cherish parliamentary institutions, to a fault. President Pica's emphasis on economic development, which he rightly sees as the best way to enrich the islands, has led to practices which some observers describe as authoritarian and which the Opposition, under the ageing Mr Ralph Baskerville, believes are only temporary.

From a diet of mutton, goat cheese and damson wine it is a far cry to the international cuisine offered at many of the big hotels. The thatched huts still occupied by the irrepressible Flongs, an indigenous people at the tip of the southern island, are generations away from the two international airports at Bodoni, the capital, and Villa Pica. Yet something of the old tradition remains and not all that has gone was worth preserving.

Like his predecessors, General Pica inherited the old antagonism between descendants of the original Spanish and Portuguese *colons* and those of the later English arrivals, sometimes humorously derided as the semicolons. Under the inspiration of his regime, those feuds are forgotten.

Wealth has made it possible to solve, for the time being, San Serriffe's most acute physical problem. Early explorers placed the islands as much as three hundred miles further west, and recent research has shown that they were almost correct.

The constant erosion of the western coasts, with corresponding accumulation on the east, is a process which, unless arrested, will bring the Republic into collision with Sri Lanka. (Bodoni, now in the centre of the north island, Upper Caisse, was originally a port.) As an expedient, lighters make the daily journey from the new wharf at Port Clarendon, built by Costains, to take the shingle from the eastern coasts and put it back where it belongs.

Wealth – and again it is the key word to anyone interested in San Serriffe – is itself creating more wealth for the islanders, particularly for those highly-placed in the administration. By making the islands a tax haven and creating duty-free zones around Port Clarendon and Bodoni all governments since that of Colonel Hispalis, which took office soon after independence, have attracted much hot and some questionable money to the islands. Once there it has tended to stay. A number of large British companies are known to be interested in exploiting this aspect of San Serriffe's financial profile.

In almost all the social and public services San Serriffe is much in advance of comparable countries, with three geriatric teaching hospitals and a pioneer pre-school psychiatric unit attached to the university at Perpetua.

The university itself has begun to acquire an international reputation for its work on thermonuclear fusion and other alternative energy sources. And the schools are attempting a unique synthesis of the old and new so that in addition to mainstream subjects a San Serriffe teenager may well be offered pearl-diving as an 'A' level choice.

British policy towards the Republic is described by the Embassy as 'basically letting the chums get on with the show'. General Pica's Government is firmly allied with the West, to which his surprisingly powerful air force is a source of comfort in a difficult area of operation.

He has been known to ask, however, whether the West is firmly allied with him.

Western governments are aware of the fragile nature of previous administrations and, while not obviously avoiding any overt involvement in local politics, would not be disinclined to do business with a successor, should General Pica wish to lay down the mantle of office. Of that, however, there is no sign.

Taylor the parodist is in his element. Anyone who has contributed to a Special Report will rejoice to see a word such as 'bounteously' which gets few other outings in journalism. The essence of meaning-less padding is enshrined in the sentence 'Yet something of the old tradition remains and not all that has gone was worth preserving.' The piece also shows how the sudden, last-minute move from the Atlantic helped to sustain the illusion in readers hoodwinked by the spoof. They were much less likely to be acquainted with the Indian Ocean and much more inclined to believe that unusual things might happen there.

San Serriffe caused a sensation, partly because of its scale but more because it pitched at just the right, uncertain level of credibility. The good-hearted, credulous readers accepted it naturally. But thousands of sceptics also wondered: could it just possibly be true? Once the hoax was realised, people settled down to enjoy the sheer cleverness of the articles and the advertisements. There were scores of jokes within jokes and invitations for people to join in. Motions relating to the politics of General Pica were put down in the House of Commons and the European Parliament. A file on San Serriffe was added to the library in the Foreign Office's weekend retreat at Chevening House. The investigative journalist Mark Hosenball, an American who was fighting deportation for breaches of the Official Secrets Act, announced in that night's London *Evening Standard* that he had finally agreed to go – to San Serriffe. The Home Office actually delayed the already endless proceedings just to check in case his spoof destination was real.

Enthusiasts were inspired to their own heights of inventiveness. A fan in Houston, Texas, drove around for four years with San Serriffe diplomatic plates. A statistician at Liverpool University invented a game based on the islands, politely acknowledged by the *Guardian*'s circulation director Brian Connor with a note which managed the best *Guardian* misspelling yet of the islands' name in its pay-off line: 'PS I enclose our only remaining San Serriffee car sticker.'

Always slightly self-conscious about the 'special' nature of the *Guardian*, readers competed both to be in on the great joke early, and to keep it going for years. Another letter arrived on 2 April from the San Serriffe Liberation Front, which had already organised a proper letter heading and plausible address. Naturally, the SSLF was furious about the pro-government slant of the special report. Many other letters debated the finer points of San Serriffian matters, enlivened by the paper's consistently unreliable spelling of the islands' name. A Friends of San Serriffe was established in Welwyn Garden City, an address which gave inexplicable satisfaction. Its 'life president' Brian Green wrote regularly to the *Guardian* with terrible puns about such matters as the islands' boycott of the Eurovision Song Contest because of objections to their entry 'Flongratulations' by the group Pica Pica Boom Boom. Ultimately, and unfortunately, plans were set in motion for San Serriffe – The Sequel, the following year.

This is the only sad coda to a story of inspiration. In 1978 a lumbering supplement of parody papers – from the *SS Times* to the *SS Sun* – greeted *Guardian* readers on April Fool's Day. They fooled nobody. Or hardly anybody – there was just one brief glorious moment when the presses in Manchester which the *Guardian* shared with the *Daily Mail* nearly folded the *SS Daily Mail* into the real one instead of the *Guardian*. Alas someone spotted the mistake in time. There was fun to be had for San Serriffe obsessives and great was the joy in Welwyn Garden City. Advertisers joined in again too, and so the essential profit was made. But apart from one or two memorable headlines such as 'Dropped Bucket Led To Romance for Innocent Topless Goat Girl', contrived under pressure by my colleague David Ward in Manchester where many of the layouts arrived from London in the wrong size and type, the exercise collapsed under its own weight. I can be rude because I played a bit part myself, trying vainly to find funny jokes to put in the leaden *SS Morning Star*. Reason

ISLAND PANORAMA :
above left, kwotes
coming home to roost
in the Woj of Tipe :
above right, the outskirts
of Bodoni ; right, one of
the many beaches from
which terrorism has been
virtually eliminated.

Bold expansion
in tourism

**Prepare for culture shock in the Acapulco
of the eastern hemisphere. Adrienne
Keith Cohen, Travel Editor, has been there**

Lord Wrongfont, last occupant of the British Residency. His statue
in Gutenberg Square, Bodoni, has been carefully maintained by
succeeding administrations

YOU MUST BE no holmes to see San Serriffe's truly unique attraction. This is the rivulle of lizitzee that travel overnight, arrive nights a week, from the cost coasts of those registered residential tourists arriving in their dozen at dawn in animal time camps at the Wroj coast tourist resorts at Cup Em Gutenssons, Villa Pica, and Gillsenas.

The wise visitor, however, will watch this spectacle from a safe distance — and protecting from behind glass. The expanded Century Hotel at Gillsenas is ideally situated for this purpose, every room facing the Atlantic direction, vast windows offering an uninterrupted view of this daily ritual — not to mention the necessary protection.

For the cargo that is unloaded with such ceremony each morning is the sand eroded the previous day from the west coast beaches by tidal currents and dumped without so much as by-your-leave along the less developed east coasts of this extraordinary archipelago.

No islands in the world can surely claim a greater population mix than San Serriffe. Just stroll through Bodoni, the capital, and one minute you will be confronted by a vast church, extravagantly decorated in the Portuguese Manueline style, the next you may well find yourself in an Arab souk. With luck (or a good guide) you can manage to take the exit from the bazaar that is guarded by an ancient Spanish fort, its walls shored up in the nick of time by a team of visiting conservationists.

In the country where the population of 1,782,000 comprises of Europeans and mixed races: Flongs, Creoles, Malaysians, Arabs, plus a leavening of Chinese, it seems only right and proper that it should have been an international expedition that managed to preserve so much evidence of the improbable history of these islands.

Spanish, Portuguese, and British by turn, they became independent in 1967. The usual upheavals followed until the current President, General Pica, restored peace and guaranteed prosperity almost overnight by declaring the islands a tax haven in which all and any foreign capital would be welcome.

The result constitutes a fair degree of culture shock.

Access

5224 910 25434 23

VALID
1265 FROM 01/77 UNTIL END 12/78

MR JOHN WILLIAMS

Acceptable currency in San Serriffe has changed
a bit in the last ten years.

prevailed and San Serriffe sailed off into history, apart from a short retrospective some years later, annual cheeps in the letters column and occasional twitches such as this *Guardian* Country Diary by Colin Luckhurst:

SAN SERIFFE [Mis-spelt again . . .] After the year round cool temperate climate of the Scottish Borders it takes some days to acclimatise to the semi-tropical temperature of these beautiful islands and the heat, together with jet lag, contributes to a feeling of light-hearted lethargy. Since our visit last year the remarkable coastal erosion which has attracted the interest of geologists from all over the world has continued unabated. From our camp-site at the head of the dunes we have ample opportunity to watch the considerable tidal scour which removes a large portion of the beach, together with any incautious bathers, on every ebb. In the banana groves behind us the remarkable contractor bird is at the peak of its nesting season. Unique among avians, a single pair of each flock is responsible for the construction of nests for the remainder, and the advance migrants, an industrious pair of splendidly plumaged birds, toil from dawn onwards in the construction of a row of nests which will be occupied by the remainder of the flock when they arrive from their long trans-oceanic migration. The people of the isles, noted for their amiability, are far from pure-blooded Polynesians. The incidence of fair hair and blue eyes bears adequate testimony to the genetic legacy of the generations of Scandinavian sailors who called here when the islands were a seasonal base for the southern whaling fleet. A widespread addiction to a form of schnapps distilled at best from pineapple and at worst from banana skins is probably to be traced to the same northern influence. Its convivial effect is said to be not only alcoholic but also hallucinatory.

Geoffrey Taylor stayed with the *Guardian* until retiring in 1991, writing the second volume of the paper's history as well as witty leaders and reflections from the strange sub-post office he ran in Littondale in Yorkshire – 'via Skipton' as he always put firmly in his address. I remember calling occasionally, muffled up against the weather, and getting the impression, until I was recognised by him or his wife

18   THE GUARDIAN Friday April 1 1977

SAN SERRIFFE

Faces in focus

The Leader of the Opposition, Mr Ralph Baskerville, arriving at the National Assembly. Below, their late excellencies, Colonel Hispalis and General Minion, who briefly held the office of President.

The leader's rise to power

General Pica is essentially a family man, a quality reflected in his choice of Ministers. Profile by MARK ARNOLD-FORSTER

FOR THE LAST 14 years San Serriffe has enjoyed stable government, rising prosperity and freedom from strikes of any kind. This happy state of affairs is largely and widely attributed to the personality of the President, Maria-Jesu Pica.

The block vote which resulted in industrial peace

JOHN TORODE discusses the rare degree of harmony between San Serriffe's trade unions and the multinational companies operating there.

ADVERTISEMENT

The People's Republic of Warrington extend joyous greetings to San Serriffe.

We the FREE peoples of the Republic of Warrington and suppliers of VLADIVAR VODKA to San Serriffe SALUTE the people of San Serriffe on the occasion of their glorious independence day.

ALEXEI RUNCORN
Beloved Father of the People's Republic of Warrington.

Janet, that customers were a suspicious interruption rather than the point of the exercise. Perhaps a similar visit by the Yorkshire creators of television's *The League of Gentlemen* inspired the comedy's famous creation the Local Shop. Geoffrey's long-distance commuting to King's Cross also had echoes of Philip Davies's mysterious comings and goings in the advertising department. But two years after San Serriffe, Davies was no longer there. His urge for a deal took him first to the boardroom of the Mirror Group, where he tried to buy the strikebound magazine *Reveille* for £1. They refused, so he poached most of the staff and started a successful rival called *Revue* and built up Europe's biggest empire of free magazines linked to companies. Selling this at a handsome profit, he turned his attention to Barrow-in-Furness where he bought the *North West Evening Mail*, the first of a chain of 19 newspapers from Carlisle to the Isle of Wight which he sold in due course for further millions. In 1992 he stood for Parliament as a Conservative against the Labour Cabinet minister John Cunningham in Cumbria, Copeland, almost achieving a sensational upset by taking over 43 per cent of the vote. If only 1,000-odd electors had chosen differently, the House of Commons would be a more interesting place.

Gerry Taylor retired to Oxfordshire where he has on his desk a framed map of the islands presented by grateful colleagues. And San Serriffe itself remains constantly able to spring back into life; indeed it helped the *Guardian* out of a tight political spot. In 1999 the paper's environment correspondent John Vidal flew to Seattle to cover the WTO summit. The meetings were besieged by anti-globalism protesters and there was serious violence. Security was tense. To his horror, John found that he had been issued with diplomatic accreditation papers rather than media ones. On the spur of the moment, he filled them in as Hon. John Vidal, Economics Minister of San Serriffe. 'No one batted an eyelid,' he recalls. 'Fellow delegates were politely interested and I discreetly passed on the latest news about the islands' trade and development.' Was General Pica still in charge? John no longer remembers.

OUT OF THIS WORLD

STERLING JEST

There are many curious names in England's West Country, from Piddle Trenthithe to Nempnett Thrubwell via Woolfardisworthy which tricks visiting tourists because you pronounce it 'Woolsery'. So viewers of the region's independent channel Westward TV in 1973 had few suspicions about Spiggot, a hamlet with whose April Fool's rebellion against the recent introduction of decimal currency was given generous coverage. The programme's quaint rustics attracted many phone calls and letters of support. Once again a Fooler had struck a timely nerve. Spiggot and its doughty folk were studio inventions, but their supporter in faraway Bradford, who said that if the city went decimal she would shop in Halifax, was genuine.

COMRADE CAPITALIST

As the former Soviet Union thawed, its sense of humour warmed up. In 1992 the *Moskovskaya Pravda* newspaper guyed the country's increasingly passionate embrace of capitalism with news that the city was going to build a second Underground system. The Moscow Underground, built by Stalin to impress the rest of the world, is a genuine wonder, with marble floors, classical pillars and even chandeliers, but it does get crowded. The newspaper explained, however, that the new system was not intended to relieve the crush. It was ideologically necessary under capitalism to have at least two of everything, 'to destroy monopolies in the interests of competition'. *Pravda* is Russian for 'truth' which this was not.

ALL GREEK TO ME

The Greeks got in on the act in 1995 at a very high level when the country's Ministry of Culture had a giddy moment on April Fool's Day. They announced that workmen excavating for extensions to the Athens Underground had found the tomb of Socrates deep below the Acropolis. Supporting evidence that it was the great man included scraps of clothing carbon-dated to between 400 and 390 BC and, most tellingly of all, a goblet with traces of hemlock. The prime

victims of this hoax were the staff of the highly reputable news
network Agence France-Presse, who reported the great discovery with
their usual dispatch, and then had to send out a retraction just as
quickly.

SHIP AHOY

It was a sight too good to miss. So a blustery April Fool's Day in 2001
saw a crowd of several hundred gather in the wind and rain on Beachy
Head to watch a full-size replica of the *Titanic* steam past. In spite of
foot-and-mouth restrictions on much of the surrounding land,
enthusiasts from up to 40 miles away managed to get to the grassy
slopes above the famous lighthouse. They were responding to an
enthusiastic bulletin on Southern FM radio. Alas, they had failed to
note a string of giveaways including the fact that the replica had been
built by the AFD Construction company. The DJ might as well have
added that she was heading for San Serriffe. Nothing steamed past but
the hoodwinked ones left their mark. So many congregated on a small
patch that a crack developed in the cliff and several days later,
fortunately when no one was around, a chunk slid off and crashed
into the sea.

VIRTUAL PARADING

In the same way that San Serriffe has lasted, the annual April Fool's
Day Parade through New York has established a sort of permanence.
The best kind; as April the first approaches, year after year, no one in
the Big Apple has any idea what will happen. This is because the
parade was a figment of the imagination of Joey Skaggs, an
accomplished hoaxer, who first announced the parade in 1986. The
only place it happened was in his head, but the notion was taken up
gleefully by many others and is now part of the city's official calendar.
Programmes, events and reports afterwards are always fictitious. Last
year, for example, the Grand Marshal was supposedly President
George W. Bush. The alleged route, should you want to organise a
float or some marching bands yourself, is between 59th Street and
Washington Square Park.

COUNTRIES OF THE MIND

San Serriffe was big enough at seven broadsheet pages, but Tom
Gleisner decided to turn his April Fool country into an entire book.
The result saw sales of over 350,000 for *Molvania: A Land Untouched by
Modern Dentistry*, which brilliantly guyed the Lonely Planet and Rough
Guide type of travel book. Decorated with a twinkly peasant whose
beam revealed awful teeth, the guide appeared in 2004 and contained
such recommendations as 'Molvania is a very beautiful country now
that radiation levels have dropped to acceptable standards.' Advice on
manners warned that in restaurants you had to pay extra for a waiter
with a moustache. The book didn't hit the funny bone of Keith Vaz, a
Labour MP and former Minister for Europe, who felt it was too cruel
to emerging Eastern European countries (Molvania was sandwiched
between Romania and Bulgaria). Undeterred, Mr Gleisner followed
the book the next year with another on Phaic Tan, a South-East Asian
hideaway whose name has to be said aloud to get the point. A San
Sombrero, rather tamer than San Serriffe, recently followed.

LET BIGONS BE BIGONS

Scientists who deal in protons and neurons and every other sort of -
on didn't think twice when *Discover* magazine revealed the existence of
the 'bigon', though if you say the word aloud a few times, you may
smell a rat. The subatomic particle also seemed to have evaded
previous discovery by nothing short of miraculous powers, since it was
said to be the size of a bowling ball. The explanation according to
Discover's April issue in 1996 was that bigons appear for only fractions
of a second before dissolving into smaller pieces. The details were
provided by a Professor Albert Manqué, suspiciously described as 'a
physicist of the old school' and based at the dubious Paris Centre de
l'Etude des Choses Assez Minuscules (centre for the study of quite
small things). Many readers spotted the spoof straight away but others
didn't and you can find the bigon appearing and disappearing on
plenty of current websites. Some believe that it was responsible for the
still unexplained collapse of the walls of Jericho. Perhaps it will in due
course be joined by the forgon, bringing invented islands, villages
and particles to a conclusion.

THE BEST EVER

Experts on fooling, students of hoaxes and polls of the rest of us
regularly produce lists of the top April Fool's of all time. Here's a
selection. All are described in detail in this book.

THE MUSEUM OF HOAXES
1. The Swiss spaghetti harvest
2. Sidd Finch, the amazing baseball player
3. Sweden's home-made colour TV
4. Taco Bell fast food buys the US Liberty Bell
5. San Serriffe

UKTV GOLD CHANNEL SURVEY IN 2006
1. The Swiss spaghetti harvest
2. Burger King's burger for left-handed diners
3. The M3 zebra crossing
4. Tesco's whistling carrots
5. Shutting the internet for cleaning

TOP FIVE APRIL FOOL GADGETS
1. Telephone cleaning compressor which forces air down wires
2. Sweden's stocking-powered colour TV
3. ThinkGeek's computer with gerbil cage incorporated
4. Virgin's mobile phone with reverse layout for left-handed users
5. Audio recordings of ancient Greece discovered by Belgian scientists
    in 5,000-year-old vase

WAINWRIGHT'S WONDERS
1. The Swiss spaghetti harvest
2. Google Earth's aliens
3. The *Independent*'s bogart picture
4. San Serriffe
5. On-screen bugs infesting computers at Queen's University, Ontario

6

The Broadsheets

Come, give us a taste of your quality.
SHAKESPEARE, *HAMLET*, ACT II SCENE II

*a*PART FROM A HANDFUL OF SAINTLY FIGURES, EVERY JOURNALIST I HAVE EVER MET SUFFERS FROM THE PUSH AND PULL OF THE TRADE'S TWO CULTURES. One is the genuine desire to tell the truth and get everything right. The second is the urge to grip the readers by the throat or anywhere else which ensures attention, and give them a cracking yarn. The first usually has to be cultivated, the second is instinctive. The two may obviously conflict and frequently do.

But they can also be reconciled, and that is where the secret of the best broadsheet April Fool's has always been found. My favourite quote from the *Guardian*'s lustrous history is not C.P. Scott's 'Comment is free but facts are sacred' but a line from the obituary of Sylvia Sprigge, a distinguished correspondent in Germany and Italy before and after the Second World War. Acknowledging her occasional gaffes, the paper nonetheless described them as 'heroic' and added 'even when her reporting was inaccurate in detail (and Sylvia could be alarmingly cavalier about dates, names and other mundane facts) it was often *penetratingly true in substance*' (my italics). Her ebullience and enthusiasm gave her reporting its edge. It is relevant but almost always overlooked that the great Scott qualified his dictum: 'Achievement in such matters is hardly given to man. We can but try, ask for pardon and there leave the matter.'

Phew. And 'phew' is the right word to encapsulate the relief and boyish excitement with which even the most dignified of British newspapers greet the approach of April the first. At last a chance to play, drop the sanctimonious pants and ignore the Reader's Editor and Code of Conduct for 24 happy hours. In the first half of the 20th century a certain social stuffiness limited these frolics but after the spaghetti harvest the grip loosened and it has been abandoned altogether since San Serriffe.

Mind you, there are a few sombre figures still roosting in broadsheet offices who watch with disapproval and they represent a significant historical tradition. For them, fundamental values are being trifled with and a covenant with the readers tossed aside. A surprising spokesman is the usually light-hearted Michael Leapman of *The Times* who attacked his own paper in a column in 1992 four days after it had run an admittedly clunky spoof about the coming abolition of Belgium. Leapman saw nerds and clumsiness everywhere. He denied being a killjoy because there was 'no joy to kill, no jokes to take' in journalists' April Fool's. He went further than showing a professional funnyman's disdain for rivals, suggesting that Belgium's communal divisions were as bitter as Northern Ireland's and not for the world's then most respected newspaper to jump about on in Wellington boots. In the end, he more or less morphed into a sterner version of C.P. Scott, concluding his piece: 'A paper's stock-in-trade is truth, a fragile commodity, hard to establish and often harder to recognise. God knows, enough lies and inaccuracies creep into the public domain by mistake, without our adding to them on purpose.' A plague on April Fool's.

This was an attitude also encountered as recently as 2006, by the merry staff at the *British Medical Journal* who carried out a well-camouflaged April Fool about a new study whose findings suggested that 'extreme laziness may have a medical basis'. The journal's genuine, and respected, correspondent Ray Moynihan reported from Sydney that Australian doctors had isolated a condition which they called Motivational Deficiency Disorder or in the inevitable initials used by medics today MoDeD. The spoof followed exactly the unexciting layout of the *BMJ* and included faithful details of a remedy

Scientists find new disease: motivational deficiency disorder

Ray Moynihan *Sydney*

Extreme laziness may have a medical basis, say a group of high profile Australian scientists, describing a new condition called motivational deficiency disorder (MoDeD).

The condition is claimed to affect up to one in five Australians and is characterised by overwhelming and debilitating apathy. Neuroscientists at the University of Newcastle in Australia say that in severe cases motivational deficiency disorder can be fatal, because the condition reduces the motivation to breathe.

Neurologist Leth Argos is part of the team that has identified the disorder, which can be diagnosed using a combination of positron emission tomography and low scores on a motivation rating scale, previously validated in elite athletes. "This disorder is poorly understood," Professor Argos told the *BMJ*. "It is underdiagnosed and undertreated."

Professor Argos is an adviser to a small Australian biotechnology company, Healthtec, which is currently concluding phase II trials of indolebant, a cannabinoid CB1 receptor antagonist. Although still unpublished, the preliminary results from the company's phase II studies are promising, according to Professor Argos: "Indolebant is effective and well tolerated. One young man who could not leave his sofa is now working as an investment adviser in Sydney."

David Henry, a clinical pharmacologist at the University of Newcastle and long time critic of pharmaceutical marketing strategies, says that although he appreciates that some people with severe motivational deficiency disorder may need treatment, he is concerned that the prevalence estimates of one in five are inflated and that ordinary laziness is being medicalised. "Indolebant

ALEX & IRAÁ/STONE/GETTY IMAGES

"People have an absolute right to just sit there"

may bring some relief to those with a debilitating form of MoDeD, but common laziness is not a disease. People have an absolute right to just sit there."

Professor Henry has organised a conference at Newcastle University to highlight what he describes as "disease mongering," which will take place 11-13 April 2006 (www.diseasemongering.org). The conference will produce a consensus statement to be published in *PLoS Medicine*,

which will launch its theme issue on disease mongering this week.

A study of the economic impacts of motivational deficiency disorder estimates the condition may be costing the Australian economy \$A2.4bn (£970m; €1.4bn; \$1.7bn) a year in lost productivity. This has prompted calls from industry and advocacy groups for a fast tracking of the regulatory assessment of indolebant in Australia and worldwide.

□

and the inevitable opposition from rival medics. The magazine owned up to the hoax the following week but by then it was too late for many respected broadsheets, which had failed to carry out basic checks. However superficially convincing, the article was strewn with clues: the main doctor was called Leth Argos, the remedy was cannabis-based and the accompanying photograph of a man napping at his desk had the suspicious caption (quoting one of the theory's alleged opponents) 'People have an absolute right just to sit there'. Yet the editor of one of the caught-out papers which picked up the tale and ran it as genuine news, the *Dominion Post* in New Zealand, had the gall to lecture the *BMJ*: 'Credibility is hard-earned. You damaged yours and ours as a result.'

As well as cheek, you may consider this to be breaking a gadfly on a wheel, on a par with the assertion by the barrister F.E. Smith, later Lord Birkenhead, that every Christian in Europe was hanging on the outcome of the Welsh Disestablishment Bill of 1914, which prompted a great satirical poem by G.K. Chesterton: 'Are they clinging to their crosses, F.E. Smith?/Where the Breton boat fleet tosses, Really Smith?' But the Leapmans were in the majority in the British quality press for almost the first three-quarters of the 20th century. April Fool's hoaxes existed but they had to sneak into subsidiary columns or modest nooks. They were hardly ever central. When they were, they were disguised with a subtlety which even their detractors could accept as an intellectual *jeu d'esprit*, a genuinely scholarly exercise.

An example was the affair of the New Keats Poems, two sonnets discovered by *The Times* in 1918 and published to a mixture of excite-ment and suspicions that they might be a hoax. The controversy roused the mischievous mind of Ian Colvin, a leader writer on the rival *Morning Post* and a skilful parodist, who gleefully composed two more false 'Keats sonnets' of his own. He added a forged letter from the poet describing how they came to be written, as conclusive proof that they were kosher. Colvin researched Keats's known movements at the time, found contemporary writing paper and employed an expert counterfeiter who produced a masterly product. This was then scrunched up, stained and hidden in a book about the poet. The plotters recruited a London bookseller whose customers included a wealthy Keats enthusiast. He would certainly buy the book and be over the moon to find the new poems which he would then undoubtedly take to *The Times*.

It worked; and the letter was also examined at the British Museum where it was authenticated as genuine (possibly by another scholar who, in the small world of London literati at the time, may have been in on the plot). But alas, at the last minute before the discovery was due to hit the headlines, the bookseller lost his nerve about the possible effect on his reputation and gave the game away. Only then did Colvin's April Fool emerge from its well-hidden ambush: the second letter in each line of the two sonnets spelt out 'The *Morning Post* before *The Times*.'

Even the crustiest of Colvin's colleagues admired the deception and so did his intended victims; what painstaking preparations and scholarship lay behind the creation of a 28-letter secret message to be hidden in a convincing parody of Keats's work. The spoof had all the features of one of its scientific counterparts which caused temporary chaos at the Massachusetts Institute of Technology in Boston. Some of the brightest minds in the world celebrated April Fool's Day there by rewiring the lift buttons, so that pressing One took people to the fourth floor and so forth. Needless to say, this is very much not a trick that the ordinary flat-dweller should imitate at home.

The lift travellers were baffled and maybe in a few cases irritated, but the ploy was essentially victimless. The *Morning Post*'s attempt was also harmless; there might have been red faces at *The Times* but the acrostic was so clever that the world at large would certainly have said: there but for the grace of God go I. This was to become a third guiding light for quality newspaper April Fool's: as well as being scholarly and if possible hidden in secondary parts of the paper, they should not cause serious distress. A final rein on too much exuberance was the modest size of even the broadsheets. For the first third of the century they would regularly be only eight pages long, sometimes six. Wartime and the long aftermath of paper rationing could make them smaller still. Modern journalists' laments that there is too little room for their masterpieces in newspapers which often stretch to more than 120 pages seem odd in this context. But if anything was to be squeezed out in *The Times*, *Telegraph*, *Guardian* or *FT*, it would be inconsequential titbits like the April Fool.

Until the *Panorama* spaghetti hit the fan, such japes as there were obeyed these rules and broadsheet editors were as cautious as maiden aunts about risking their hard-won reputation for reliability and trust. Attempts to run convincing spoofs were met on several occasions by editors reminding junior staff of the reaction to the BBC's first known hoax, an imaginary description of a mob storming Parliament and blowing up the Savoy hotel in 1926. How this got past the scrutiny of John Reith in the troubled year of the National Strike is a mystery I have not yet solved, but it led to the jamming of the infant corporation's switchboard, emergency cables to the Admiralty and panic as far away as Newcastle upon Tyne whose Lord Mayor was asked what defensive measures he was taking. This was despite the fact that the broadcaster, the Catholic priest Ronald Knox who was also *Punch*'s leading parodist at the time, had larded his work with warnings that it was airy persiflage. As well as straightforward announcements that the item was fictional before, after and in the middle of the broadcast, the 'riot' involved such unlikely revolutionaries as a Mr Popplebury, described on air as general secretary of the National Society for the Abolition of Theatre Queues.

So a gentle era of fitful pranks reigned for some 50 further years in the upmarket press, interrupted only by journalists' private word games which saw secret attempts to smuggle agreed words such as 'phrenological' or phrases like 'I was wild' into print. The writer Hilaire Belloc was also a hack journalist who loved this kind of thing. He kept a record of how many times the expression 'Mark my words!' appeared in print and analysed the relationship between its use and the user later being proved a ninny. By 1930 he had a list of 157 major and 2,372 minor entries of politicians and other prophets using the phrase in print. Only 418 had escaped what he called 'the irony of God falling upon them later like a ton of feathers or an obliterating fall of snow'.

An extended version of such word games was sometimes licensed on 1 April to include what are known in the United States as 'mountweazels' after a fictitious entry in an encyclopedia for an American photographer called Lillian Virginia Mountweazel. A former fountain designer, she was born in Bangs, Ohio, and died aged only 31 in an explosion while on assignment for *Combustibles* magazine. Not.

Such tiny ambushes are sometimes inserted in expensive reference books for copyright reasons, to prove that a rival has simply lifted material, but they are also the stuff of broadsheet tomfoolery which has left a legacy all over the world. Membership lists of Germany's Bundestag often include Jakob Maria Mierscheid, a non-existent but extraordinarily active politician who has chaired the parliament's committee for small and medium-sized businesses and sings in the choir of the wood and plastic workers' trade union in between updating his seminal work on bird migration. Music critics have sometimes ill-advisedly picked up on the coining in 1903 of the equally dodgy name Zzxjoanw, meaning a type of Maori drum. Fans of such spoofs get extra pleasure from discovering them and then telling others in a knowledgeable way that, for instance, the letters Z, X and J do not exist in the Maori alphabet.

It was a combination of prosperity, ample newsprint and the social liberation of the late 1960s which finally reintroduced the whole-hearted April Fool to the quality press. *Panorama* showed the way and where the spaghetti pointed, others began to follow, encouraged by the merciless rise of satire as the old Establishment crumbled amid fiascos like the *Lady Chatterley* trial and the Profumo affair. Among the ultimate rulers of the *Guardian*, the Scott Trust, the impish Liberal Party leader Jo Grimond did his bit to erode excessive high-mindedness. He teased the then editor Alistair Hetherington that the paper should use two fonts of type: plain for things which it knew to be true, gothic for items about which there was even the slightest doubt. It was a joke but Hetherington took the half-serious point: there was room for a little deliberate fooling in a paper which, if it was really honest, would have to run rather a lot in gothic. All the hesitations of the past still put a brake on the process, so that when the idea for San Serriffe was raised at the *Guardian* it came from Philip Davies in his lowly role as advertisement rep for special reports, not some star writer. But the dam broke, and preparations are very different now.

Within the context of the general lightening-up of Britain, the fantasy islands taught two mouth-watering commercial lessons to senior newspaper executives. April Fool's was absolutely up the street of bright young advertising agencies and their wealthy clients, and they had the potential to bring free publicity for a title all over the world. After 1977, everyone set about the annual hoax with a will. Top byliners and heads of department took charge.

The results showed in two ways. A hit or miss quality attached itself to the spoofs, with all the resources and pooled brains either pitching at just the right spot or sometimes, as in the 1978 follow-up to San Serriffe, making a meal which was too rich. The April Fool's hoaxes also began to get bigger and bigger. Two of them have just slid out of the cuttings folder on my desk and concussed the cat. One is the *Guardian for Sunday*, an enormous collection of puns and pranks which ran for 36 pages. Issued with the *Guardian* on Saturday 31 March in 1990, it took clever advantage of the fact that April Fool's Day fell on a Sunday when the paper did not publish. All the inventive power of the features department was steered into it by Alan Rusbridger, now the *Guardian*'s editor, and there were eight lucrative full-page ads, a double-page centre spread for Ford and a string of smaller advertisements all gamely following April Fool's themes. Three years later, out of the *Guardian* plopped *Ciao!*, an intellectual version of *Hello!* magazine with 12 pages including the likes of Jacques Derrida and Sir Isaiah Berlin inviting readers 'into their beautiful homes' and the same ratio of advertising as the Sunday spoof.

The *Sunday Telegraph* also entered the heavyweight spoofing league with five pages of its colour magazine on a wartime barrage balloon detachment still manning their posts at Durness in remotest northern Scotland. They had been moved there in 1944 by mistake, instead of going to Dungeness in Kent where their demob papers, suits and other correspondence were still awaiting them. The *Independent* meanwhile excelled with picture spoofs including a memorable image of an elusive new British mammal, the bogart, being trapped by a mountaineer in wellies with a noose on the end of a punt pole, against

How fortunate that a photographer was on hand to capture this rare – indeed unique – sighting of the mythical bogart, half badger, half fox, on Skiddaw in the Lake District on 1 April 1988! *Brian Duff*

the stunning backdrop of the Lake District fells above Keswick. The piece also included the membership card of the British Bogart Preservation Society. This was an unusual, indeed possibly unique spoof: an April Fool in one sense but also a true story.

It hit the headlines after a noted North of England photographer called Brian Duff, who was working for the *Daily Express* at the time, called in at The Twa Dogs pub in Keswick in the mid-1980s and was intrigued by a stuffed animal in a glass display case. The landlord Gordon Hallett explained that this was a 'bogart', a mythical Cumbrian beast sprung from the mating of a badger and a fox. That never went on in the tales of Beatrix Potter, possibly because Mr Tod and Tommy Brock preceded the days of civil partnerships, and it turned out that it hadn't gone on in The Twa Dogs either. The bogart was the creation of an extremely skilful taxidermist, but the landlord had genuinely set up a bogart preservation society and he enrolled Brian as a member.

The two of them then sallied up the foothills of Skiddaw with the stuffed hybrid and took a series of stalking photos. Alas, the *Express* had recently neutered its Manchester office and the crew on the London newsdesk had a different sense of humour. They didn't want the story or the picture. But Brian didn't forget it. When he retired after 28 years with the *Express* and went freelance, he dug the tale out again.

'*The Independent*'s use of pictures was a breath of fresh air and I thought this would be a natural,' he says now, still in possession of his BBPS membership card in retirement at his home in Burnley. 'I went back up and did a different series of pictures. It was easy. It looked wild but there was a car park nearby and then we walked across a couple of fields. I had Gordon jabbing the pole, the bogart hiding behind trees and scampering over walls, the lot.' He copied the membership card with its line drawing of two bogarts canoodling amid foliage and the whole package appeared in the *Indy* on 1 April 1988. Gordon and his regulars at The Twa Dogs were particularly pleased to be described as 'a small group of conservationists'. They also managed to hoodwink BBC *Nationwide* which did a follow-up. Gordon has since died but the bogart, badger in front and fox behind, lives on at the pub where it presides over strongman competitions, in-bar line dancing by the Keswick Kikkers and other Cumbrian frolics.

It therefore isn't surprising that if you look on websites or read overseas accounts of modern April Fool's, you will often find the British press described as one of the great production houses. But the United States has kept its end up well too. There was a splendidly pithy example from the newspaper *USA Today*, which has a very big circulation in hotels. Acknowledging that hundreds of thousands of copies would start the day lying on the floor outside rooms, it printed a bold-print banner at the top of its front page saying 'Do Not Disturb'. The *LA Weekly* in Los Angeles went to the other extreme in 1985 with an article called 'A Weekend To Remember'.

Its author Michael Dare recalled a decade later how it felt to have created 'the biggest April Fool ever' which in terms of active participants this probably was. He began his piece with a reprimand to the *Weekly*'s high-income, intelligent and sometimes bored readers:

'You stayed home again last weekend, despite the dozens of glorious and exciting things the *L.A. Weekly* told you there were to do. Well, I'm sorry, but there's no excuse for such laziness this first week of April . . .' The article then ran through a list of extraordinary events such as a free nude ballet in one of the city's parks, a day of free health care at the exclusive Cedars Sinai hospital and the fact that the Los Angeles Police Department had discovered a cache of thousands of Italian shoes and were giving them away. There were 100 altogether, run deadpan but with a large sub-heading in bold reversed type which said 'A guide to special events in L.A. on or about April 1.' Dare's finest moment came when the LAPD rang him and said 'What is it with these shoes?' He recalled: 'I took a deep breath and said the one thing I hadn't said all day, especially to a cop. I said: "April Fool."'

A few minutes' thought would have led most readers to realise or at least suspect that the guide was a hoax. But exploiting the fact that people don't do that is the whole quality newspaper April Fool game. Alan Rusbridger, who still takes a hand in spoofs such as the *Guardian*'s suggestion in 2005 that Prince Charles was to be made New Labour's countryside tsar, says: 'They work best if they're plausible enough for you to believe them when you're half-asleep.' In the sense that you have to be a bit of an anorak to wake up on 1 April and say, ah-ha it's April Fool's Day, I must be on my guard, most of us are indeed half-asleep to the prospect of the annual tricks. If you deconstruct recent quality papers, too, you soon see how much they gain from their authors' being tapped into current trends and talking points. However complex, the *Guardian*'s are rarely concocted until the last minute to make sure that they are catching the latest tide. The writing benefits too from the adrenalin of a deadline.

And so it goes on, more than ever these days. *The Times* and the *Daily Telegraph* may have withdrawn from trying to keep up Fools on a large scale, and the *Financial Times* is seldom inspired to join in. But *The Economist* dreams up weird genetically engineered gryphons and other such larks with the best of them and the reputable news agencies like Reuters usually have a crack. Democratically, media offices also draw increasingly on the wide range of talents they all have – and as we will see in Chapter 9, this applies a fortiori on the internet. I can never meet my mild-mannered and delightful colleague Roger Tooth, who heads the *Guardian* picture desk, without recalling his appearance in a chiaroscuro photograph looming from the 1992 spoof Men's Page. Having a fine moustache and a generally masculine appearance, he was hauled up to the London office's fifth floor in Farringdon Road, recently deserted by Ratner's the jewellers and presenting a suitably bleak background, to pose as the author of *Oedipus, Electra, Feminism and Me*, a coruscating attack on the women's movement in which he claimed to be 'at one with the primate within me'. Last year, the plausibility of the paper's claim that Chris Morgan of Coldplay was endorsing David Cameron's new Conservatives was given conviction by Pascal Wyse, a features sub-editor who is also a talented musician. The spoof made excellent use of the paper's website which hosted – and still does – a RealPlayer version of Coldplay's 'Talk' reworked as 'Talk to David', Morgan's absurd song of praise to the Tories.

Absurd but . . . Guess who allegedly fell for it, giving a warm glow to everyone in Farringdon Road for the rest of the day. In spite of the high-wire strategy of bylining the piece 'Olaf Priol' which was tantamount to stamping the whole exercise in red print saying 'Check out the date folks', the narks from New Labour's spin machine were apparently instantly on the case. The *Guardian* reported the next day that the party's media monitoring unit had 'faithfully disseminated the story to most of the Government without a hint of irony'. It certainly spread and so did po-faced reaction. In the States, a former Democrat congressional hopeful called Andrew Kaza announced on his weblog: 'This is no April Fool's joke' and lamented that one of his favourite bands could fall for 'a guy who has all the charm of a British used-car salesman, in my book'. The next day, the *Guardian* diary reported a denial from the Labour media guys who claimed that there hadn't even been a briefing to ministers on April Fool's Day because it fell on a Saturday '. . . and we spent all Friday night in the pub.' Who do you believe? asked the diarist Jon Henley, hitting once again on the question at the heart of all April Fool's.

TRICKS FOR TOP PEOPLE

ROUND THE CLOCK

It had the virtue of simplicity: in 1991 *The Times* revealed that the relatively new but already choked London orbital motorway the M25 was to follow an alternating one-way system. On Mondays, Wednesdays and Fridays all six lanes in both directions would be used clockwise. On Tuesdays and Thursdays everyone would go the other way. The idea was given credibility by the usual assortment of technical details plus the fact that things would revert to normal at weekends. Hoax protesters were soon joined by real ones as readers rang or wrote in. It rapidly became impossible to tell who was genuine or otherwise, among opponents including a Labour spokesman who claimed that many drivers already had problems distinguishing between left and right (this at a time when the big political parties were beginning to meet at the middle ground). Likewise suspicion attached to a commuter from Swanley in Kent who said: 'Villagers use the motorway to make shopping trips to Orpington. On some days this will be a journey of two miles, and on others a journey of 117 miles. The scheme is lunatic.' Congestion has since become so severe on the M25 that the apparently mad scheme may now seem like a bright idea.

TUM-TI TUM-TI TUM-TI TUM . . .

Two quality outfits got together in 2004 to mount a joint spoof, BBC Radio 4 and *The Independent*. Their target was the daily comfort-saga of middle England, *The Archers*. Once midnight had marked the end of 31 March, the series' makers announced on their section of the BBC's website that the time-honoured theme for the programme was to be remixed by the electronic musician and composer Brian Eno. The news was shared exclusively with the *Indy* which carried the story to readers' breakfast tables. The story was well wrapped up in Beebspeak about the story of everyday farming folk gradually reflecting a more diverse slice of Britain. A tune of rustic jollity was therefore no longer deemed appropriate. Eno had been given a brief to create something cooler, more urban and reflecting modern Ambridge's 'racy hotbed of affairs and scandals'. Eno pitched in with a vigorous attack on the existing tune as 'reactionary, exclusionary and failing totally to address the concerns of young people'. Outraged calls to the BBC's duty officer and the *Indy*'s switchboard were encouragingly numerous.

NIGHTMARE AT BROADCASTING HOUSE

The BBC wasn't let in on the *Guardian*'s 2004 spoof, and several executives admitted heart-stopping horror when they saw the headline: 'Mandelson tipped to take over at Broadcasting House'. The great resigner of New Labour politics was revealed as the front-runner to be chairman of the corporation when Gavyn Davies retired; and he had plenty of plans. Enough of these were credible, including a determination to protect the BBC from the disruptive influence of the oppositional left, for much more dubious material to sneak through the defences of sceptics. Although Mandy is fond of dogs, it might seem unlikely that his manifesto included pressing for the BBC to feature live coverage of the whole of the Cruft's dog show. Enthusiasm to investigate the London property market was also a bit of nudge-nudge, after Mandelson's disastrous mess-up over borrowing money for his grand home in the capital. Finally, the jokers risked another heavy hint linked to familiar photographs of the politician relaxing on his Charles Eames chair. His BBC would carry a three-part retrospective on the great man's ground-breaking furniture. In spite of all this, at least one rival's night news editor, whose job included checking the early editions, left a memo for the day-desk saying 'This may be an April Fool but I can't be certain.' An official at the Department for Culture, Media and Sport also admitted to the *Guardian*: 'For seven seconds, I thought, Oh f***.' The job actually went to Michael Grade.

APRILTRIX

Real people are often enlisted in April Fool nonsense, as happened with the eminent archaeologist Professor Barry Cunliffe of Oxford University in 1993. He has discovered many things but the peak of his career was revealed by the *Independent*, which reported that a genuine unconquered village of Gauls had been found by the Prof. at Le

Yaudet, near Lannion in France. This is exactly where the author René Goscinny sited the dauntless village of his Roman-bashing hero Asterix. Cunliffe's find, aided by Dr Patrick Gaillou of Brest university (another genuine expert, on Brittany), included a circle of standing stones, as endlessly chiselled by Obelix, and coins with the image of Asterix's favourite food, wild boar.

HOT AIR FROM PLANTS

Would you believe in a plant called *Solar complexus americanus*? Possibly, but surely not if its discoverer's name was Professor Olaf Lipro. Still, a lot of normally canny Scotsmen forgot the date in April 1995 and fell for the Glasgow *Herald*'s account of this heat-generating wonder plant. Its great virtue was that if you watered it with three pints a day it gave off as much warmth as a 2 kW electric heater. Entirely submerged in water, a bed of several Solars would heat enough water for showers, baths and central heating in local homes.

BRITAIN RULES THE SKIES

Dreaming of a white Christmas was declared at an end by the *Guardian* in 1981 via a report that scientists at research labs in Pershore, part of Worcestershire previously associated only with fruit-growing, had discovered how to control the weather. This was a slightly laboured but archetypal scientific spoof, enjoyed more for all its in-jokes and learned quips rather than genuinely catching anyone unawares. Needless to say, it painted a golden picture for Britain which was set for permanently warm long summers with rainfall confined to nighttime. The rest of Europe would get whatever the meteorologists in Pershore decided to send it. Christmases would always have snow, added the project's leader Dr Chisholm-Downright whose dishevelled photograph was almost as unconvincing as his name. He was shown gloating over a computer printout forecasting more sunshine in Pershore and blizzards in Marseilles.

RANDY CRITTERS

It seems a while ago now, but around the millennium the sex-revitalising drug Viagra was the talk of the town. *The Independent* duly struck on 1 April with details of a version for pets. Given the genuine stash of absurd products for cat- or dog-obsessed owners, this seemed entirely likely, even if most animals seem to spend their entire lives thinking about either sex or food. The *Indy* sailed close to the line with a paragraph claiming that there were few things as sad in the world of pets as a guinea pig – those non-stop breeders – sitting in its hutch thinking 'I haven't had sex for months. Am I so unattractive?' But wavering credulity among the spoof's victims was boosted by realistic instructions for using the pill which was branded Feralmone.

SEEING DOUBLE

The *Toronto Star* seemed to have scored with a high-quality spoof in 2004 when it invented a detailed April Fool about new regulations for local joggers. The city council had come up with a by-law forbidding speeds of over 10 kilometres an hour. Going any faster made too much noise, in the way of grunts and trainers slapping on the tarmac, for the local black squirrels to breed successfully. The only problem was that Westdeutsche Rundfunk in Cologne got there first; 11 years earlier. The radio station convinced a goodly number of German joggers in 1993 that 6 mph was the new speed limit – to safeguard sensitive mating procedures among the parks', yes, squirrels.

CELEBRITY SNARES – FOOLING WITH THE FAMOUS

☺ **Britney Spears** was the subject of a spoof on 1 April 1999 when the Wall of Sound website 'revealed' that she was 28, eleven years older than her actual age of 17. The piece was prompted by a raunchy cover picture of the teenager on the cover of *Rolling Stone* magazine, and was crammed with genuine-sounding personal detail. Names were given of schoolfriends of the singer who could bear the claim out and hundreds of anxious fans called Spears's record label to beg: 'Tell me it ain't true.'

- ☺ **Prince Charles's** office rang BBC Radio 4 to ask for a copy of the supposed new Euro-anthem broadcast in German in 1999 as a replacement for 'God Save the Queen'. Staff later said that they had only been playing along to keep a good joke going.

- ☺ **George Clooney's** Hollywood friends are always on the alert on 1 April, a precaution which reached a climax in 2005 when rumours flew round Tinseltown that the actor was hiring friends to pose as police officers and arrest a very famous film star. Nothing happened in the end and Clooney said gnomically: 'Amateurs party on New Year's Eve and pull pranks on April Fool's Day.' But this too has been interpreted as a trick to lower victims' guard next time round.

- ☺ **Liz Hurley** was given a special retraction in the *Guardian* in 1995 after readers took seriously an April Fool column in her name, headed 'Tired of lingerie, tired of life'.

- ☺ **Lord Steel** was targeted for an April Fool in 1993 by, of all unlikely institutions, the Serious Fraud Office. A wag involved in the investigation of an allegedly dodgy businessman faxed a cod letter of support from the former Liberal leader as part of a police in-joke which led to grovelling apologies and red faces all round.

- ☺ **Vanuatu** the miniature Pacific island nation narrowly avoided a severe economic crisis in 1996 when its government signed IOUs for £65 million in exchange for promises of profits in a non-existent development scheme. Fortunately the letters of credit were discredited, because of their prominent date stamp of April Fool's Day.

7

The Tabs

'Ha! ha!' quoth he, 'full plain I see . . .'
SAMUEL TAYLOR COLERIDGE, *THE RIME OF THE ANCIENT MARINER*

i WILL NEVER FORGET MOVING AS A YOUNG REPORTER IN 1977 FROM THE LONDON *EVENING STANDARD* TO THE *GUARDIAN*. It was like swapping a drink-fuelled playpen for the cloisters. Riotous days started early on the tabloid, often after I had phoned over a theatre review from a public kiosk in Maida Vale wearing a cosy fleece-lined anorak over my pyjamas. Once, I remember with glee, this happened from the relative luxury of a room at the Shakespeare hotel in Stratford-upon-Avon where my views were much helped by listening through the wall, with the help of the traditional glass pressed against the plaster, to Michael Billington phoning his review to the *Guardian* late the previous evening.

We were cunning on the tabs, but also professional in the matter of actually getting our stories and finishing them quickly, to a degree which seemed remote to my new colleagues in broadsheet-land. Trained to ring in with a check call to the newsdesk once I had filed my copy from the great outdoors (into which *Guardian* reporters seemed to venture much less often than *Standard* ones), I soon gave up this practice because it was met with polite surprise. The main reason was trust. *Guardian* recruits had been selected, interviewed and appointed and could therefore be left to get on with it. You sent off your copy and the next day it appeared, sometimes with added misprints in those days of capricious hot metal.

Weaving truth with trust, in the phrase of one of the grand mottoes on the frieze in Leeds Town Hall, was not what the 20th-century British tabloids were about; certainly not in their early years which repeated all the blithe confusion between fact and fiction which marked the American press in the 19th century. An interesting witness for the prosecution is Henry Williamson, author of *Tarka the Otter* and *Salar the Salmon*, who went so far as to write a memoir called *The Confessions of a Fake Merchant* about his spell at the end of the First World War working for the *London Weekly Dispatch*. This was a time when music halls resounded to a skit on the Drunken Sailor which included the lines: 'Some of it's truth and some of it's lying/Who cares a bean if the public's buying/Journalists never leave off trying/Early in the morning.'

Williamson certainly never left off trying. For some of his brief career in Fleet Street he was a 'space-reporter', not a specialist on the stars and planets but a penny-a-liner paid to fill the gaps between real news. He invented a dramatic rescue of a dog trapped beneath the Blackfriars railway bridge on Ludgate Hill by a man standing on another man's shoulders on top of a double-decker bus. He brought a fictional porpoise up the Thames several times, depending on how much or how little real news was going on. He admired a colleague who created a completely fictional 'honeymoon colony' of tents set up in Sussex by desperate young couples, to add colour to a piece about the serious issue of homelessness in London. Rivals scoured the Downs and were baffled not to find it. 'These harmless stories were easy to do,' said Williamson who was tickled to discover before he abandoned journalism for writing in 1921 that the *Weekly* actually had a Fiction Editor.

Williamson never claimed the credit, if that is the right word, but he also inspired an internationally famous piece of fooling with an on-the-spot brainwave when the *Weekly Dispatch*'s editor hauled him in for missing a story scooped by rivals. 'But I have a better one,' he said, with instinctive tabloid guile, and he spilled out a farrago about a rare peregrine falcon setting up home in St Paul's Cathedral and slaughtering the famous London pigeons. He had seen the killer bird himself, on his way back to the *Dispatch* office from reporting a Communist Party meeting in Cannon Street. Crowds had been gaping skywards . . .

It went down a storm, to the extent that Williamson was able to enjoy accounts for months in other papers of the exploits of the non-existent hawk. And this is exactly what happened in Chicago a few years later, when the city went wild over a splash in the local *Journal* about a chicken hawk settling at the city's Art Institute and decimating *its* famous pigeons. Fraud has never actually been nailed, although no one but the original reporter ever saw the bird, but the story led to a celebrated series in the *Journal*, 'The Pigeon and the Hawk', which was the San Serriffe of its day. Initially taken seriously, it gradually turned into a citywide in-joke as everyone of any note in Chicago appeared, thinly disguised, as supporting actors to the fearsome predator and its endlessly wily prey. Other imaginary hawks subsequently appeared in other cities, followed in more recent years by real ones. A pair of peregrines started roosting in Derby Cathedral in 2004 and fledged their first three young in 2006. Williamson's ability to weave fact with fiction served him well when he found his real calling, as a proper writer. Indeed he managed to fictionalise his newspaper fakery in a novel called *Innocent Moon* which was based in part on his *Weekly Dispatch* shenanigans. But where was the place for April Fool's in the year-round farrago which he had left behind in Fleet Street? For some years to come, that was a pretty pointless question. Another witness of the harum-scarum world was James Bone, the long-serving London editor of the *Manchester Guardian* who maintained high standards of accuracy himself but much enjoyed the company of his rascally red-top rivals.

Bone had left school in Glasgow at 14 but was from a family brimming with talent. One of his brothers, Muirhead, became a sought-after artist, the other, David, was commodore of the Anchor Line's enormous merchant fleet, and both were knighted. James himself became a Companion of Honour. He was a genuine Fleet Street legend and a man who portrayed the foibles of London life with great skill and humour to his Manchester clientele. One of his favourite characters was a journalist he called 'the stunt man' – stunt being a relatively new coining in the trade for a half-truth embroidered into a newspaper story. Bone described on one occasion how a desperate contributor of 'pars', small fillers for the popular press, went to send a letter from a post office and noticed that the pet cat on the counter was sitting with its tongue out. On a whim, he gave it his stamp to lick which it did. The next day a very short story appeared under the headline: Post 'Office novelty – Stamp-licking cat of Charing Cross'.

Like the best April Fool's jokes, this was to girdle the Earth. Not only was the post office besieged by punters wanting to send catlick mail (until the cat was driven demented and fled after two days) but the story spread and resurfaced for years. Animal protection societies weighed in, MPs spoke and the innocuous prank took off. Bone's friend was sent clippings from across the country and, as the years went by, from Australia, Shanghai and the United States. Fresh details were often added; the cat became 'coal black' and was given other distinctions. The journalist who set the whole thing going, at a time when he was getting very little in, became a prankster emeritus. Another of his stunts, recorded Bone, was the discovery of a sparrows' nest in the dusty legal shrine of the Temple made entirely out of red tape. I should add that Bone never gave mundane details about the stunt man, such as his name, age, newspaper, etc.; but even if a composite his report was penetratingly true in substance (see page 83).

This could have gone on for ever but it didn't. The tide turned during and after the Second World War, when the effect of unbridled lying by the propagandists, especially the Nazi machine created and led by the former journalist Joseph Goebbels, sobered reporters up. It was not exactly the beginning of an age of virtue, but popular papers such as the *Daily Express* under Arthur Christiansen and the *Daily Mirror* led by Hugh Cudlipp adopted serious agendas, often investigative and campaigning, and pursued them brilliantly. In doing so, they established a convincing tone which came to mark the tabloid spoof when it re-emerged in the era of San Serriffe for an annual outing at the beginning of spring.

Christiansen was the king of the scoop and exercised iron control over his underlings; he once bawled out the Northern editor for an hour after the *Express* used Garamond type for a headline in the

Manchester edition instead of the usual font. Cudlipp was the man for stirring controversy. Their different talents each had a part to play in cleaning up the stunt artists' legacy while allowing April Fool's their place provided that they were done well and went for appropriate targets.

As far as Christiansen's skills were concerned, an April Fool is by its very nature an exclusive, although there have been odd occasions when foolish minds have thought alike. On 1 April 2005, three popular newspaper cartoons in the United States, *Foxtrot*, *Pearls Before Swine* and *Get Fuzzy*, all ran a more or less identical line of three frames in hundreds of papers worldwide from the *Washington Post* to syndicated customers in South America and Europe telling the same ouija board joke. One of them later admitted collaboration, saying 'This is the sort of thing that happens when cartoonists get too little sleep and then talk on the phone.' The other distinctive feature of the majority of tabloid pranks is the 'up yours' approach to authority in which Cudlipp specialised. While the quality papers fanny around with their subtle parodies, the hard newsmen pick an Establishment target (today it may just as likely be the 'New Establishment' of vacuous celebrities or footballers' wives) and belt it. The Queen goes to the bookies. Gypsies occupy Windsor Great Park under a forgotten 13th-century law. Blair paints Downing Street door read. Stick in the democratic pin.

The creation of these pranks was, and is, helped by the convivial nature of tabloid offices where larks and japes are more common than at their quality counterparts. The London *Evening Standard* always put on an in-house pantomime at Christmas, full of Lord of Misrule quips about the editors and management, and there were many covert internal games. In the *Standard*'s Shoe Lane office, now history, photographs were sent from the picture desk to make-up on an overhead wire, powered by a spring and with lead weights clipped to the bottom of them to help achieve speed. The only person tall enough to be hit by these missiles was Max Hastings, later editor of the *Daily Telegraph* and a knight of the realm. The picture desk would wait until he set out on one of his occasional visits to the gents which was the other side of the office, and timed their release of a lead-packed bunch of pictures with precision. Max would invariably thunder

'Hell's bells' but would always have forgotten by the next time he
needed to go.

Likewise in Manchester, until the late 1980s a major centre of
newspaper production and editorial jobs, a certain sense of anarchy
encouraged an atmosphere where wild hoaxes could be devised. At the
Daily Express one of the photographers, Jack Kay, had a pet duck which
used to accompany him to the office and the Crown and Kettle pub
next door, where it had its own pan of water while Jack drank his pint
of Bods. In the office, the duck lived in a developer tray in the
darkroom, on one occasion narrowly escaping a throttling from the
paper's Northern editor John McDonald who was showing round a
party of potential advertisers. As he described to them 'the most
modern darkroom in any newspaper office in the country', Kay's duck
couldn't resist quacking from the corner where it and its tray had been
hidden. Such absurdities were a fertile context for April Foolers
dreaming up the annual prank.

Excellent, snappy spoofs duly followed. But as with Pandora's box,
a trouble-making sprite turned out to have escaped, as well as all the
bright ideas. The old disregard for fact-checking and taking basic
precautions re-entered tabloid newsrooms as staff were cut and competition hotted up in the 1980s and thereafter. The sense of joy
admittedly spread by the *Sun*'s entirely fictitious front-page splash
'Freddie Starr Ate My Hamster' had its less life-enhancing and also cir-
culation-damaging side. Tabloids have become prey to falling for other
people's spoofs and it is never very impressive for a fooler to be fooled.

Last year the *Sun*'s Bizarre column on showbiz and celebrities
reported that 'Brit Kate Beckinsale is the latest actress to be linked
with the role of Wonder Woman', supplemented with a little salivating
at the prospect of 'Sexy Kate' in a tight-fitting superheroine's dress
after her recent success portraying a sultry vampire. It wasn't a major
story but its origins are interesting and of course these days they have
been exposed and made permanently available on the internet. The
story existed originally only in the minds of slightly desperate April
Fool's Day pranksters at a film news website called JoBlo which ran the
exclusive on 1 April. It dropped an assortment of heavy and salacious
hints about Beckinsale needing a 'boob job' for the role and the

director Joss Whedon – a well-known feminist and creator of the feisty Buffy the Vampire Slayer – talking about actresses offering to 'blow him' for the part. It even finished by saying that he had agreed to play along with JoBlo's 'annual April Fool's Day gag this year, which was a nice thing of him to do, especially since that's what you've been doing by reading this entire article.' The *Sun* clearly didn't get to the end.

Or rather other global media didn't; because the spoof was first picked up and filleted by others such as the World Entertainment News Network, the Internet Movie Database and InTheNews, zooming across the wide-open prairies of the internet and losing all the original giveaways while gaining embellishments as it spread. Oh crikey. Mind you, in incautious moments or when working at speed – the main reason why all claims for absolute accuracy in journalism must be treated with suspicion – we can all tread this path.

Imagine my glee when I chanced on an online reference to an article in the *Sun* headed 'Captain of the flagship' and apparently describing Debo Adesina's reign as editor of the *Guardian*. In great excitement at this apparent transcultural link between the tabs and the qualities – my own paper, what's more – I fed Debo Adesina into anagram engines. The 131 results from Adenoid Base to Idea Nose Bad didn't seem fool-related and when I finally tracked down the full article I discovered why. It was a workmanlike interview by Joy Chinwokwu of the *Daily Sun* ('Nigeria's King of the Tabloids') with Mr Debo Adesina, the editor of the *Guardian* ('One of Nigeria's most sizzling and dependable news magazines'). Sadness; except it was worth it just to find that excellent marketing slogan 'sizzling and dependable' which might sum up tabloid journalism at its best. And guess what; for coincidence freaks, Mr Adesina was taken on by his *Guardian* as a reporter on April Fool's Day 1988 and made editor on April Fool's Day 11 years later.

'Surely, an interesting coincidence!' writes Joy. 'In fact, if I were him, I would have assumed (and I told him so), that someone was pulling my legs – offering me a job and promoting me to the height of my profession, on April Fool's Day. Amidst a hearty laughter he says, "There is something about April Fool's Day and me but I think it was just a coincidence."' Ha, ha indeed. Full plain.

TABLOID TRICKERY

THE ELECTRIC BRAS

It was slipped in quietly on a minor news page, but the *Daily Mail*'s April Fool on rogue bras in 1982 scored very well on the gullibility register. It was the brainchild of the reporter John Passmore who used the real name of a friend's business in London and a cast of its actual employees to bolster his story of how 10,000 items of the underwear were being recalled. The problem was that the extra-supportive bras had been wired with a spare supply of specialised copper alloy originally intended for use in fire alarms. Alarm bells should always ring in April when unusual or specialised materials are mentioned, but the article had some alluring pictures of blonde women having their bras tested with monitors, and these may have lulled sceptics. The wire apparently gave off static electricity when it came into contact with nylon and body heat, as bras do. This then caused interference with radio and TV broadcasts. The story caused mild embarrassment for women at work on the day, notably at British Telecom whose chief engineer went as far as asking research and laboratory assistants to check what type of bra they had on.

EYE IN THE SKY

The *Sun* needed only 144 words to concoct an April Fool in 2004 which has made many of the Best Prank lists. It was very simple but nicely illustrated and with a typical punning headline: 'The Long Arm of the Claw'. Reporter John Coles crammed his limited space with a heroic number of bird-related puns as he described how Thames Valley police had fitted speed cameras to hawks which would swoop above drivers on the M40. Motorists squawked with rage, the hawks were part of a flying squad, the speeders were easy prey, the birds were talon-ted. The pictures showed a tiny but sinister dot in the sky and a hawk's eye view of speeding cars. Their mini-cameras (developed by BBC wildlife teams) could make out not only the speedo but also registration numbers and details of tax discs. PC Otto Hergt (a name which needs deconstructing) called the hawks 'a valuable new weapon' but motorist Alan Payne had the last word. The scheme, he said, was bird-brained.

MARATHON MAN

Heroically lost or misdirected outposts are an April Fool stock-in-trade, like the wartime barrage balloon which the *Sunday Telegraph* claimed to have discovered in Scotland. In 1981 the *Daily Mail* tracked a Japanese runner who had misunderstood the rules of the London Marathon, held on 29 March, and thought that he was supposed to run not for 26 miles but for 26 days. The man's name Kimo Nakajimi had nice echoes of being knackered and gyms and readers were asked to look out for him on suburban roads or in the Home Counties. Sightings were included along with an admission from a marathon organiser, Timothy Bryant, who confessed that his Japanese was dodgy and that Kimo might also have been confused because of 'the very long races they have over there', a nicely vague phrase.

SOCK HORROR

The *Daily Mail* tapped into a hot discussion topic in 2000 when it announced that a new sort of sock had been invented which helped people lose weight. Well aware of its readers' profile, it craftily added that the range would be available through Esporta health clubs where *Mail* men and women determined to be lean and fit are often to be found. The socks had the disadvantage of sounding absolutely disgusting. They had the in-your-face name of Fatsox and promised to suck fat out of sweating feet. The usual po-faced cod science explained that a patent polymer called FloraAstraTetrazine had been adapted from previous use in the nutrition industry by a Professor Frank Ellis Elgood needless to say from the United States. The word Flora had margariney connotations which added to the spoof. Professor Elgood explained that as a gym-user's body heat rose and their blood vessels dilated, the socks drew 'excess lipid from the body through the sweat'. You then washed the stuff out afterwards, although this could also be done by the au pair.

AMERICAN SPAGHETTI

I have to mention this one although it leaves me cold, because Americans rank it up there with *Panorama*'s spaghetti harvest. In 1985 *Sports Illustrated* in the States carried a cover story on a baseball discovery, Sidd Finch, who could pitch a ball at a completely extraordinary 168 mph. Lightning speeds have become commoner in the 20 years since then, for example in the grunt 'n' whack world of Wimbledon tennis, but this was at least 70 mph faster than any other player of the American version of rounders had managed before. Young Sidd was on trial with the New York Mets and had a completely incredible background of training with Buddhist lamas in remote Tibet etc. But he tapped a sentimental national nerve and has become a byword for comic genius, exercised in this case by a witty sports writer called George Plimpton. Other sports journalists were soundly hoaxed, abetted by the Mets' pitching coach Mel Stottlemyre – no anagram there, promising though the name seems – who played along briefly with the story and its cunningly staged photographs of Sidd practising.

TUNNEL VISION

If you're spoofing the building of a tunnel there's one enticing joke to play and the *News of the World* went for it in 1990. The paper reported that the Channel Tunnel project, at long last under way after centuries of discussion, had run into yet another glitch, and a really bad one. Costs had already spiralled and labour troubles had added to engineering challenges to slow things down. Now, guess what, surveyors had realised that the two halves being built simultaneously from Britain and France would miss one another by 14 feet. The £10 billion error – previously used as an April Fool on tunnels in the Alps, America and Japan – was blamed in proper tabloid style on French engineers who had insisted on using the metric system. The Brits had stuck loyally to miles and inches. Other Chunnel spoofs over the long years of construction (1987–94) included a more original suggestion in the *Sunday Express* that work had stopped after the discovery of a gold seam at exactly halfway which was being claimed by both Britain and France. The *Daily Mail* was also in on the act by discovering a sealed-up tunnel from the Napoleonic era, wide enough to let a donkey through and designed to rescue French aristocrats from the guillotine.

MOG MOCKS THE BEEB

The *Daily Mail* rang the changes in 1977 when it launched a hoax competition to mark April Fool's Day, rather than attempting any spoofery
of its own. Well in advance of 1 April, readers were invited to spill the
beans on their wickedest pranks. It was an early example of the sort of
interactive, reader involvement journalism which has since become
all the rage. Interestingly, the winners highlighted one of the perils of
precisely this: the fact that there will always be some naughty readers,
listeners or viewers who take the media for a ride. It's happened with
my own paper; I know at least one wildly exciting venue listed in our
travel section's 'Tell us the best places in . . .' slot actually exists only
in a practical joker's mind. Ditto with the *Mail*'s winners, the Morron
brothers of Liverpool. They won for entering an entirely imaginary
benefactor called Mog Edwards (named after the character in Dylan
Thomas's *Under Milk Wood*) for Radio 4's Man of the Year contest. Mog
came 12th in 1971, sixth in 1972 and second only to Enoch Powell in
1973. The brothers' serious point was to show how few people voted
in the contest (just as today's bloghorrhoea attracts unimpressively few
comments). Mog's second place was achieved with only 173 votes.

ONE WISHES TO PLACE AN EACH-WAY BET ON . . .

The black arts which picture editors can now use to alter photographs
came to the aid of the *Daily Mail* in 2004 when they decided to
celebrate April Fool's Day with a royal picture exclusive. The package
drew cleverly on discussions at the time about the birth of 'citizen
journalism' – the way that digital cameras, especially those combined
with mobile phones, had the potential to turn anyone into a reporter
if they happened to be at the scene of a newsworthy event. So it
seemed in the case of an Austrian tourist in London who had got
brilliant snaps of the Queen, surrounded by her trademark corgi
dogs, visiting the bookies William Hill in person to place her Grand
National bet. The reporter Paul Harris explained that the Queen
liked to do this in person after an aide placed a bet on the wrong horse
and lost her a few hundred pounds in winnings. That had happened
way back in 1969 but cunning use of a headscarf and dark glasses
meant that her cover had never been blown. The pictures were the

winner, however. One showed the Queen outside the bookies with her copy of the *Racing Post*, studying the latest Grand National odds in the window. The second, realistically blurred, was of her actually placing her bet at the counter. As Mr Harris said, choosing his words carefully, they were 'truly incredible'.

APRIL FOOL AND OTHER DISHES

No good at practical jokes? Then why not try whisking up some April Fool or trying other items in this easy-to-follow cooking section?

Basic: Serve a meal backwards, starting with pudding. If you have Chinese family members or guests, avoid soup, because in China they serve this last anyway.

Easy: Dye an entire meal blue. Good ingredients/dishes are vichyssoise or cauliflower soup; cod in white sauce with mashed potato and leeks; ice cream; iced water and/or white wine. Add blue food colouring liberally to everything and make sure you have a secret snack earlier. The effect on taste buds is dreadful.

Traditional: recommended for April Fool's Day by *A Kitchen Witch's Cookbook* from a 17th-century English brew which 'inspires thoughts of spring frolic, abundant buttercups, and pranks by the Fey'. Take:
4 hard-boiled egg yolks
$\frac{1}{2}$ cup sugar
$\frac{1}{2}$ cup softened sweet butter
Pinch of fresh thyme or 1 tsp.
Ditto sweet basil
2 tbsps. orange flower water
1 lb cooked noodles
1 sliced orange
Beat the egg yolks, sugar, butter, thyme, basil, and orange water in a

small bowl until smooth. Mix enough of the butter with the hot noodles to coat them with a golden-yellow color. Garnish with orange slices.

Haute cuisine: A two-course feast with two tricks. Quantities should serve four.

Starter: Ravioli al Pesce d'Avrile.

You need:

500 grams of sliced fish

1 clove of garlic

Parsley

Milk

Two slices of white bread

400 grams of egg pasta in sheets

1 chilli pepper

Butter

Parmesan

Chives (or spring onion)

Extra virgin olive oil

Salt

Ready, steady, cook:

Chop the garlic and brown it in a small amount of oil in a frying pan. Add the fish in little pieces and cook for a short time on a high heat. Soak the bread in the milk, drain, and add to the chopped fish together with the garlic and some chopped parsley. Season with salt and form into a paste. Spread the pasta and use the fish paste as a filling to make little parcels, or ravioli, of whatever size you like. Put the chilli in one of them. Cook them all in boiling water, keeping the one with chilli in a separate pan to be served to the friend(s) who are going to be the April Fool. Drain and serve with melted butter, chives and parmesan cheese.

Apparent main (but really it's the dessert . . .)

Fishy pie

You need:

Puff or shortcrust pastry (ready-made is fine)

Rhubarb

Sugar

Cloves

Egg glaze

Raisin

Ready, steady, bake:

Lightly flour work surface and roll pastry into an 11" _ 16" rectangle.
Use knife to cut out two similar-sized fish-shaped slices. Place one on
baking sheet lightly dampened with water and press edges to stop
shrinking. Dice rhubarb, add sugar and cloves, simmer until tender,
then drain and place along centre of fish. Cover with second fish,
damping joins all round with water and pressing firmly together. Press
all round with end of fork. Put in fridge for 15 minutes and preheat
oven to 220 degrees. Brush top of fish with egg glaze and after two
minutes use knife or plastic straw to make seriously realistic 'scales' and
decorations to suit. Cut smiley mouth and press in raisin for eye. Bake
for 20 minutes and further 15 on lower heat if necessary until
scrummily brown. Serve with vanilla ice cream disguised as mashed
potato and cream with dash of green food colouring and scraps of
angelica for parsley sauce. Add sacrificial peas or salad garnish for extra
effect.

A-level: hard work but good if you want to get even with faddy kids.
You need:

Lemon jelly

Kit Kat bar

Golden-coloured cracker biscuits

Vanilla ice cream

Caramel syrup

Dehydrated peas and carrots

Ready, steady, scam:

Make jelly and pour into glasses, sticking a straw in while it sets. This is
now lemonade.

Crush the cracker biscuits into small fragments. Break the Kit Kat into
sticks and coat them with cooking spray. Dust with the shattered

bikkies. These are now fish fingers. Spoon the ice cream on the plate and top with caramel (if necessary adding brown food colouring to the latter). Hey presto! Mashed potato and gravy. Add the dehydrated veg (or still better sweets shaped like carrots and peas or best of all rubber ones). Say you have to go to the loo but 'Start anyway kids' then creep outside and take photographs through the window.

8

The Advertisers

Take all the fools out of this world and there wouldn't be any profit.

JOSH BILLINGS, 1818–85

IN A GUILELESS MOMENT, YOU MAY BE THINKING THAT THE MEDIA DREAMS UP APRIL FOOL'S EVERY YEAR TO ADD TO THE GAIETY OF THE NATION AND GIVE US ALL A HARMLESS BIT OF FUN. This is true up to a point, but that point is very soon reached. When the *Guardian*'s San Serriffe team held their secret meetings with the J. Walter Thompson advertising agency everyone was thinking about the same thing. Money. And so it came to pass. The paper's circulation lifted only slightly on the day, because news of the great spoof came too late for extra copies to be printed, but the supplement's advertisements raised a handsome sum. How much? 'I'm not sure that anyone could work that out so many years later,' says Philip Davies. 'But let's say that I met my budget target very early indeed that month.'

Let's say, by 2 April. San Serriffe was advertisement-rich to an extent which only the supplements commissioned in their entirety by the North Korean dictator Kim Il-sung could match. Four out of the seven pages were taken up with advertising. But it was advertising of an interesting, and at the time mould-breaking, kind. Amid cloak-and-dagger precautions to avoid leaks of the impending prank, copywriters were let in on the secret and all their talents were let rip.

Some of the best jokes in San Serriffe are in the ads.

Thus you can read a quarter-page explanation from Guinness of why their stout in San Serriffe has a white body and a black head, an upside-down version of the real thing. Beneath a convincing photograph of the drink in both a bottle and a glass, the text explained how this anomaly came about.

> It was after the freak barley crop of '56 that the local inhabitants of San Serriffe first began to notice a change in their beer.
>
> The taste was the same. It still poured slowly and evenly. But the white head turned out black, and the strong dark body was white.
>
> Experts put it down to the novice farm helpers who spent their holidays in San Serriffe that year. Knowing little about crops, they sowed the barley seeds upside down . . .

And so it went on, describing how the unique Guinness had been an island secret for 20 years, now at last to be broken by the first-ever export of bottled upside-down Guinness to the United Kingdom. Then followed a forerunner of today's sophisticatedly interactive spoof advertisements, with their answerphone messages and links to film or audio on websites. The drink would soon be available in pubs and clubs but *Guardian* readers could be the very first to try it if they sent off for a free conversion kit. Thousands did, dutifully obeying the instruction to put the coupon upside down in their envelopes for 'easy sorting' at the firm's Royal Park brewery.

Kodak announced a competition for the best holiday snaps of the islands, Shloer fantasised in a comic strip about the 'Compacta' subtropical apple and in the 'old *Guardian*' tradition of cardigan and sandals, the 'People's Republic of Warrington' in Cheshire sent fraternal greetings in true Kim Il-sung style. This quarter-page ad came from noted funsters Vladivar Vodka, whose drink is distilled in Warrington and whose copywriters showed a nice line in pastiche. Their lyrically turgid parody noted how 'Already the half-built spire of the People's Museum of Diesel Transport casts a welcome shadow over the former mansions of the Warrington aristocracy.' Even the workaday word 'welcome' is beautifully placed there.

How San Serriffe
turned Guinness upside down.

It was after the freak barley crop of '56 that the local inhabitants of San Serriffe first began to notice a change in their beer.

The taste was the same. It still poured slowly and evenly. But the white head turned out black, and the strong dark body was white.

Experts put it down to the novice farm helpers who spent their holiday in San Serriffe that year.

Knowing little about crops, they sowed the barley seeds upside down.

Not until the brewing process was nearly completed did the Head Brewer discover the mistake. By which time it was too late.

Faced with disappointing thousands of loyal Guinness drinkers he took the now historic decision to continue to brew.

For twenty years San Serriffe kept their secret. Indulging themselves in a Guinness that was truly unique.

Now, to coincide with their emergence, San Serriffe has decided to export a special celebration bottle. Their loss is the world's gain.

Guinness, as brewed in San Serriffe, should shortly become available in your pub, club and bar.

You'll know it by the special label on the bottle, and of course it's instantly recognisable when you pour it out.

However, if you'd like to be one of the first to try a San Serriffe Guinness we'll happily send you a free conversion kit.

To get yours, cut out the coupon, putting it upside down in the envelope for easy sorting, and send it to San Serriffe Guinness Export Dept., 6 or 9 Turnover Strasse, Park Royal Brewery, London NW10 7RR.

The advertisements were run before the hush-hush editorial team at the *Guardian* who were full of admiration at how entertaining, for example, chartered surveyors could be. The London and Brussels estate agency St Quintin Son & Stanley invented a patron saint for San Serriffe – St Quintin of course – and a legend of the sort all patron saints have. During the shattering earthquake of 1477 he saved the capital Bodoni's cathedral by standing in, like a caryatid, for a pillar under the great south portico which was in danger of collapsing. The blurb continued with the assurance that St Quintin, in the form of the estate agents, could protect property investors in San Serriffe just as effectively. 'You'll be all too aware of the problems,' it added. 'Grasping politicians, hopelessly corrupt officials, primitive populace, obscure legal systems, incompetent local builders and many, many more.'

All the advertisers reported a bumper response to their japes, including the *Guardian*'s own fake ones for, to take one example, a position as Reader in Lunar Spectroscopy at the University of San Serriffe. Despite the fact that applicants were asked to enclose a small bribe and advised that much of their work would involve extracting energy from moonbeams, people sent in their CVs. Tim Radford, a contributor to the spoof and letters editor at the time, recalls one hopeful starting his application: 'Although not a lunar spectroscopist . . .' and going on to ask if there were any other posts available on the campus.

Now all this was noted eagerly in the advertising agencies of Soho and the marketing suites of British and international companies. It was a grand but respectable realisation of dreams and wheezes which had a disreputable past. Grab your garlic and wooden stake because we are turning to the dark side of April Fool's here. Bring along a copy of Vance Packard's *The Hidden Persuaders* and a couple of DVDs of *Absolutely Fabulous* for good measure.

We can blame the Americans to some extent. The black magic of the publicity stunt was perfected over there by men like Harry Reichenbach who publicised some of the earliest blockbuster films such as the Tarzan series with fake stunts. His most successful involved paying a gang of New York urchins to crowd round a Brooklyn art gallery and grimace, point and make smutty remarks about a tasteful but not very distinguished nude by a second-rank French painter called Paul Chabas which was on display in the window. An anonymous phone call tipped off the authorities and the painting, *September Morn*, was threatened with confiscation and the furnace in a court case for obscene publication. Everyone was acquitted to acclamation and *September Morn* prints have since sold by the million; people recognise the teenage girl stepping modestly from the sea in her birthday suit even today. The marketing guys created *September Morn* dolls, umbrellas, calendars, statuettes, tattoos and walking stick heads and Reichenbach rejoiced. Some years later there were rival newspaper hoaxes about the fate of the comely young lady; some (including Chabas) claiming that she was a happily married mother with three lovely children, others that she was a prostitute in Paris.

The commercialisation of April Fool's in the US in the 1920s and 30s reached ridiculous lengths and one of the better ones took the mickey out of the way things were going. After a run of pretend suicides by beautiful starlets in a lake in New York's Central Park, all to publicise their movies by faking tragic love affairs, a nightclub entertainer called Mary Louise Guinan took a hand. She invited reporters to the park where an obvious dummy was being hauled from the water. When quizzed about who it was, she replied surrealistically: 'It's me. I did it because I loved him.'

The British were soon copying. With breathtaking bad taste, a chancer called Arthur Vectis Freeman, better known by his more dynamic-sounding alias of Frank Power, publicised a forthcoming film about Lord Kitchener by claiming that the great man's body had been washed ashore in Norway and was about to be brought home. The public were not spared unsavoury details of the tragic corpse's burial and disinterment and there was a more serious side. The British Admiralty finally issued a report on the tragedy which saw the ageing cruiser *Hampshire* hit a mine in the North Sea in 1916 and go to the bottom with the Commander-in-Chief. Power actually turned up at London docks with a coffin but was met by the police instead of cinema-going crowds and arrested when the coffin was opened and found to be empty.

Adapting this rather sinister past to the playful world of April Fool's was right up British admen's street but interestingly it was a German company which first made a name for successful repeat hoaxing. The poor Germans suffer from a largely undeserved reputation for plonking humour; at some stage in the dispersal of the Angles, Jutes and Saxons, all the subtle ones are often held to have sailed off to Yorkshire where they settled down and invented irony and riddles. There may be some truth in this, but let's give the *Berliner Illustrirte Zeitung* of I April 1934 its due. It wasn't exactly a hilarious time in Germany, but the newspaper's story and photograph of a man flying with a machine powered by his own lungs was a corker.

It may have been in the minds of two BMW executives, Tim Greenhill and Peter Kinnaird, when they met in the post-San Serriffe world with an up-and-coming young adman, Robin Wight. To adapt the famous slogan of their rivals at Audi, the car-makers were playing with the idea of *Gemütsstimmung durch Technik* or Humour through engineering. This was the basis of the flying lungster and BMW adapted it in 1986 for a series of April Fool advertisements which continues to this day. Every year produces a just-credible refinement to the luxury saloon's range: an inaudible beam which gives hedgehogs enough warning to jump onto the verge; a computer gizmo which allows the returning motorist to take control of their cooker at home and make dinner.

Like the car itself, the ads may seem a little bulky and obvious, but readers of the quality papers in Britain, and a number of other markets including Canada where different versions have appeared, fall for them time and again. This is in spite of the fact that they feature on almost all lists and websites about April Fool's and BMW's own education division carries encyclopedic details about them in responses to its list of Frequently Asked Questions. Duncan Forrester of BMW reckons that the 'background' context of more or less all-the-year-round advertising for the brand lulls punters into thinking 'oh, another BMW ad', and then getting drawn in by the notion of dual controls for Continental driving or the Egyptian Pharaoh-influenced 'Toot 'n' Calm Horn' which allays road rage. The innovations usually have a close connection with real, or at least realistic, car improvements and include interactive response systems – phone lines to dial or web pages to visit – which enhance the joke but also (we're in the cold-blooded world of commerce, remember) monitor customer numbers and brand response.

The BMW ads have remained the playground for Wight's agency, one of those outfits whose staff have accolades such as winning top place in a poll by *Esquire* magazine about the world's 'most sought-after purveyors of original thought'. Wight himself has become a guru of this world although he had one setback. In the general election of 1987 he fought the Labour stronghold of Bishop Auckland, County Durham, for the Conservatives and was shown the door. Here too there were echoes of San Serriffe, whose original creator, the *Guardian* adman Philip Davies, also tackled a hopeless Northern seat for the Tories. Unlike him, Wight saw the party's vote slip and Labour's majority in Bishop Auckland go up by more than two-thirds.

The question of April Fool fatigue, as tackled by Duncan Forrester, applies on a wide scale to spoof ads nowadays, particularly as weaker marketing brethren get in on the act. A trawl through the internet sites of advertising and PR agencies soon shows how everyone has latched on to a niche which Philip Davies originally had almost to himself. Thus one commentator exults in how 'brands have leveraged April Fool's Day – not all of them worked creatively but who cares if every newspaper and TV station has your brand all over it? That's marketing paradise that is.' Ironically the same chap praises the day as one of the few not taken over by rampant consumerism like Christmas or Mothering Sunday. At this point, consult your copy of *The Hidden Persuaders*.

Another observer in the US enthuses: 'April Fool's Day is a great day to lie and get away with it' – adding an emoticon smiley ☺ – 'And your lies will create some buzz before they are busted. And if the people are really shocked with the lies and believe them, the buzz will be even bigger after the lies have been busted.' I was plunged into deep thought by this, especially as I had just been chatting on the phone to my relatively saintly colleague Oliver Burkeman, an April Fool composer for some years, who told me: 'No journalist wants to wake up in the morning thinking: Ha, ha, ha, I tricked the readers.' Just think; there are people who are even less scrupulous than us.

But it certainly works for them; and the adguys are particularly well aware how we the consumers can be softened up by gently self-mocking spoofs. These have a long and sometimes distinguished history; the comic artist William Heath Robinson made his name through drawing advertisements which showed his trademark mad machinery at work in the service of companies as varied as Izal disinfectant, Standard fireworks and Meccano toys. Guinness had a brilliant run of joke ads in the 1950s and 60s, and at the time of writing, I go to the cinema mainly in the hope that the mobile phone network Orange will be showing a new advertisement in the series which beautifully sends up the company itself. Podgy and otherwise repellent Orange ad execs and marketers humiliate famous film folk and I have to keep pinching myself as a reminder that this is no real reason to switch from Vodafone.

America retains a major place in all this, of course. Some of the most acclaimed modern ad-Fools have been the work of the States. Fittingly for another nation often said to be low on irony, they have a simplicity which can sometimes hit the bull's-eye, as happened with the Taco Liberty Bell. The Liberty Bell is an American icon, a venerable chunk of bronze which clanged out in Philadelphia when Colonel John Nixon gave the first public reading of the Declaration of Independence in 1776. It has a famous crack which opened up when it was first rung 23 years earlier, no doubt because it had been made in London. An inscription on it spells Pennsylvania with only one 'n' but loyal Americans love it in the way that we feel fond of Stonehenge.

Well, the Liberty Bell had been targeted by spoofers once before. Not by any old spoofers either, but possibly by Phineas T. Barnum himself when the bell was taken to New Orleans under armed guard in 1884 for a Cotton States Centennial whose slogan was 'No North, No South but an Undivided Country'. A newspaper hoax claimed that the treasured relic had been stolen, complete with compelling details such as ruts left in the mud by the villains' heavily laden wagon. There was national fury, especially in the North where a Confederate veterans' plot was immediately suspected. But after the hoax was exposed and the fuss subsided, the centennial exhibition and related events had a surge of extra customers.

On 1 April 1986 the Taco Bell Corporation, whose Tex-Mex fast food could claim modern American iconic status and whose name has obvious echoes, took space in the *New York Times* to announce that the company had bought the Liberty Bell. The holy relic would remain on show in Philadelphia but would be renamed the Taco Liberty Bell, in the way that countless football stadia, hotels and institutions have been given this sort of corporate branding. The company reminded readers of the 'adopt-a-highway' scheme which allows roadside advertising in exchange for payments to maintain and clean the tarmac, and added piously: 'We hope our move will prompt other corporations to take similar action to play their part to reduce the country's debt.'

The joke was swallowed as completely as one of the company's Cheesy Fiesta Potatoes and there was outrage. Thousands of people contacted the bell's home at the National Historic Park in Philadelphia before noon, the traditional pumpkin deadline for April Foolers, when Taco Bell came clean. Goodness, were they smiling. The prank was covered by more than 650 newspapers and magazines and over 400 TV and radio stations (and continues to whirl around the world, of course, in countless references online). Within a month of April Fool's Day, Taco Bell's marketing people calculated that they had reached 70 million Americans without spending a dime beyond the cost of the *New York Times* ad. Revenue at their 6,500 outlets in the States rose by some $500,000 on the day and $600,000 on 2 April compared with income the previous week. Even President Reagan's White House lent a hand, both to Taco and another US business giant. Spokesman Mike McCurry was taxed about the apparent outrage before noon and replied off the cuff that the Lincoln Memorial in Washington had also been sold and would in future be known as the Ford Lincoln Memorial.

Taco Bell's people purred about the proof of their corporate slogan 'Think outside the bun' and with good reason, but they were perhaps on to a winner with food. Of all the countless products sold by April Foolery, food and drink come top. Another stunt usually in Top Ten lists of ad-pranks was the announcement by Burger King on 1 April 1998 that they had perfected a Left-Handed Whopper, aimed at the 32.5 million left-handed Americans (13 per cent of the population) who had suffered 'fast food discrimination' for much too long. An advertisement in *USA Today* which was soon repeated at no cost to the company around the world explained that the ingredients of the jumbo beefburger remained the same, but all the extras such as the garnish, sauce and condiments etc. had been rotated 180 degrees to make the product convenient for the left-handed to eat. There is something initially mind-stopping about this claim, as the brain struggles to work out whether rotating a burger's contents can have any effect at all. When I mention it to people, they often start by making Homer Simpsonish noises like 'Duh'. But Burger King went into considerable detail about how the shift in the bun meant that potential spillages (familiar to anyone noshing into one of these vast things) would be skewed to the left, making it harder for them to slide out of the usually dominant but for left-handers open, right-hand side.

What a whopper, eh? Shamelessly plugged, too, by Burger King's then senior vice-president for marketing Jim Watkins who said proudly: 'This is the ultimate "Have it your way" Whopper' and promised a rollout to 'other countries which have large left-handed populations'. The following day the company issued an even more self-satisfied statement describing how thousands of customers had gone into Burger Kings to ask for the new line, with almost as many wanting to make sure that they got the traditional, right-handed version. There were some complaints from frustrated left-handers but Burger King was encouraged to continue down the path of *Gemütsstimmung durch Technik*. Later 1 April ventures from BK have included the website www.subservientchicken.com which was launched without any marketing other than a little surreptitious word of mouth. In that spirit, I will tell you no more about it, except that it has had well over 20 million hits.

British consumers, in the literal sense, were treated to an awful concept by Mars sweets in 1994 when the company flagged up the 'Emperor' bar which supposedly contained 32 lbs of thick chocolate, glucose and milk. It was only on sale for one day, 1 April naturally, although it would have taken the rest of the year to eat. Mars didn't make the mistake of actually producing one, unlike the Snapple company which erected the world's biggest ice lolly in Times Square in 2005 and then watched in horror as it melted far more quickly than anyone expected. Fruit-flavoured goo threatened to leach into the subway and the fire service had to close off surrounding streets while they washed the remains of the 17-tonne, 25-feet-high monster away.

In final, virtuous contrast to these disgusting hoax advertisement excesses, let us praise the whistling carrots of Tesco which combined healthy eating with a useful way of avoiding watery veg. There is nothing more revolting than an overcooked carrot, except perhaps sprouts in the same condition, but properly managed ones are delicious and healthy. Indeed their vitamin A can do all sorts of good things, including helping our vision. This was used by the Royal Air Force in the Second World War to hide the secrets of radar in the secret war described in the account of R.V. Jones's career on pages 28–30. After the night fighter pilot John 'Catseyes' Cunningham had shot down 20 enemy aircraft, the RAF put it about that his diet of carrots gave him owl-like vision in the dark. The Germans took it seriously and so did the Brits; there was a tremendous surge in carrot-growing on allotments because people thought that eating them would make it easier to get around in the blackout.

Tesco built on this patriotic base with an advertisement in the *Sun* on 1 April 2002 which got extra attention because the Queen Mother had died the previous day at the age of 101 and hardly any newspapers or broadcasters went ahead with their own April Fool's. Terence Gibbons was working in Tesco's press and marketing department at the time and remembers the creative huddle as the wheeze was worked out. 'It was the time when people were worrying about genetically modified crops and those stories about European Union interference and mad regulations kept cropping up too,' he recalls. 'The one that sticks in my mind was some nonsense about supermarkets having to get the bend out of bananas.' Alongside that, big stores like Tesco were routinely asking suppliers for 'nice-looking' fruit and veg except in the organic section where wrinkles and blotches were fine. The fictional carrots were duly genetically modified to start whistling like a kettle when they were cooked just nicely. The secret lay in tapered airholes and the product's many virtues included its suitability for introducing children to fun but effective ways to help in the kitchen.

Gibbons has worked in a number of companies before and since his time at Tesco. He divides them into those which steer well clear because they are convinced that foolishness might damage their reputation, and those which go for fun all the year round. He says: 'We had a non-stop calendar at Tesco – Christmas, New Year, Valentine's, Mother's and Father's Day and of course April Fool's. It's just such brilliant marketing; if the joke takes off like the carrots, it's also free.' Quite by chance, the 2003 April Fool also stole a march on one of Tesco's nearest rivals. By coincidence Sainsbury's were preparing to introduce a new line of novelty, purple-coloured carrots a month later. They were genuine but whistle-weary shoppers found that hard to believe.

ADVERTISING BREAKS

DRINKING UP TIME

Conscious of their pioneering role in fun advertising, Guinness the brewers were quick to follow up their part in San Serriffe and play a leading role in the tide of April Fool's which then swept in. One of their best stunts was in 1998 when they announced a deal with the Royal Observatory at Greenwich which would lead to GMT in future standing for Guinness Mean Time. There was just enough supplementary detail for this dubious notion to survive until noon, when it became clear that the time pips were not, after all, going to be replaced with the plop of drips from a hand-pulled beer pump in a bar. The *Financial Times* got in a tizzy about this after taking it seriously and ticking Guinness off for 'setting a brash tone for the Millennium'. In a correction, the *FT* rather haughtily said that the news was 'apparently' an April 1st spoof. Unlike *The Economist* with its genetically engineered animals etc., the *FT* has kept away from April Fool's, although it did try to find out in 1977 how much the *Guardian* had made from San Serriffe.

LITTLE SILVER MAN

The entrepreneur Sir Richard Branson likes to be ahead of the game and one of his many April Fool's achieved this by happening on 31 March. The bearded one emerged at 5 a.m. from a fake flying saucer in a field on the outskirts of London in 1989, clad in a tight, shiny silver suit which initially alarmed local residents and a police officer. Several squad cars had earlier been summoned when an inflatable green extraterrestrial squeezed out of the saucer first. The contraption was a convincingly designed version of the hot-air balloons which have always fascinated Branson. He had planned to swoop into Hyde Park on April Fool's Day with news of an entire new planet, and decided to run a secret rehearsal two nights before. But the wind changed, stalled the saucer and grounded him off-target. Local residents were not amused but Branson disarmed the ones who had been genuinely scared. 'We thought that you would be tucked up in bed at that time of day,' he told them before flying off.

IT'LL NEVER FLY

Apart from arriving in London by flying saucer, the ingenuously publicity-crazed Branson has been involved in many other April Fool's. Some had an edge; in 1996 Virgin Cola announced that a new consumer-protecting gizmo in its cans meant that when the drink passed its sell-by date, the aluminium would turn blue. Needless to say, Pepsi-Cola had recently rebranded its own product in cans which were largely blue. Branson also managed a plausible one in 2002 when Virgin directed the world's attention to a journal called *Trends in Ecology and Evolution* for an account of how company slogans had been successfully imprinted on butterflies' wings. This united current public interest in saving the planet and genetic modification with a possible subliminal reference to the chaos theory phrase about the beat of a butterfly's wing in the Amazon jungle leading to a change in world weather, which millions of people including myself vaguely know about but don't understand. Virgin's marketing director John Riordan also did his bit with some genuine-sounding adbabble. 'We think advertising via butterflies is a natural synergy for an airline. We're always looking for fresh new ways to promote our products and services, and what better way than via a constantly flying medium?'

ANAGRAMS FOR THE PHARAOH

Mohamed Fayed campaigned vainly for years to become a British citizen and so naturally wanted to take part in the outbreak of annual pranking which is central to the nation's soul. Actually his idea in 2002 was a good one. After endless grief over the ownership of Harrod's department store, he was bound to get journalists biting with news of a company float. In spite of the blindingly obvious giveaway of a company contact called Loof Lirpa, plenty waited with interest for a promised second press release at noon. This announced that Harrod's would indeed float, in the form of a new branch on pontoons in the river Thames. Perhaps concerned that the Stock Exchange would take a maidenly, *FT* view of the jesting, Fayed then spoilt the joke by saying that the news was 'intended for amusement only'. Still, well tried.

GOOGLE ME TO THE MOON

Google has got plenty of mentions in this book but they are well deserved and the company's deliberate mixture of spoofs with genuine announcements about new products on April Fool's Day is fascinating. The ethos seems to run through the entire firm; I was delighted to find an email on an April the first internet thread from a Google employee saying that 'of course' the milk in his office fridge that day had been dyed green. So one more handclap, please, for Google's spoof moon base Copernicus which advertised for staff in 2004 to survey the internet from an unparalleled vantage point and answer questions such as 'Does spam go on for ever?' The job also involved harvesting faint electromagnetic pulses in a way which could re-create the lost first appearance of Pink Floyd on BBC TV. There were plenty of clues, including a preference for employees 'capable of surviving with limited access to such modern conveniences as soy low-fat lattes, The Sopranos and a steady supply of oxygen'. The base was also going to be a hideous sprawl because of the Moon's welcome freedom from 'the blight of sentient lifeforms or restrictive zoning ordinances'. But loads of people clicked the application button which triggered an auto-reply saying sorry, we're full, but try again on April Fool's Day 2104.

DUCKS, COWS, BULLS AND BEARS

Companies are sometimes wary of April Fooling because so many investors take the plunge to buy or sell first and only think afterwards. Take the example of a Canadian website which ran a spoof about Canada's capable finance minister Paul Martin giving up his job to retire to a farm and pursue his real interest of breeding rare Charolais cattle and 'handsome Fawn Runner ducks'. This excellent following of Cincinnatus' example was extremely unlikely but nonetheless appeared to cause a blip on the Canadian stock exchange. The country's dollar fell to a one-month low against its US counterpart and Mr Martin's office was forced to deny that ducks and cows were about to replace his real interest, which remained the stock market's bulls and bears.

TURNING BRIBES TO ADVANTAGE

The end of Communism led to a sprouting of infant capitalist organs in Eastern Europe. Being young and fresh they have shared little of the caution of serious Western financial papers when it comes to April the first. The Romanian specialist daily *Ziarul Financiar* for example went to a lot of trouble to devise a sliding scale of new taxes on what it called the growing national practice of paying 'commissions and supplementary insurance payments for health and a better life'. In plainer Romanian, this meant bribes to officials, and indeed the article specified that the government was considering a yardstick of creaming 5 per cent on payments of up to one million euros. Officials were also debating incentives for bribe-payers which would allow half their spending to be offset against other taxes, a way of increasing national revenue which might have earned the private admiration if not public approval of Lord Keynes.

GOING DOTTY

Sunday papers have to wait for seven years before getting their chance to play April Fool's, and the *Observer* was ready and waiting in 1979. In a direct commercial arrangement the paper teamed up with the pioneer of cheap flights, Sir Freddie Laker, to announce an amazing new travel scheme called 'Sky Dot'. Although bylined by genuinely big-hitting reporters in London, Washington, Los Angeles and Tokyo, the spoof was rather too amazing to convince anyone apart from the highly gullible or inattentive. It involved shrinking people to the size of a full stop like this one – . – and hurtling them across the world in only a minute or two on laser beams. The accompanying photograph looks ancient today, with doll-sized businessmen scattered round a Laker jet with the genial entrepreneur, full size, clutching several of them to his bosom. An early form of interactivity invited readers who wanted to be first in the queue for Sky Dotting to send in a coupon which prudently included the words: 'I accept that the *Observer* can not be held responsible in case the project is not realized.'

PARKING IN PILES

The Mini enhanced its appeal to Australians in spite of their vast open spaces and predilection for equally big camper vans, via an April Fool in 2003. The little car's makers claimed to have found a way of ending parking misery by a system of 'vertical parking locators' which stacked the runabouts one on top of the other. Attached to the sides of existing buildings, the slim and stylish car lots had enough genuine precedents to make them at least feasible. If you visit the unadulterated 1960s nook of Bond Court in Leeds you can see a rare example of a vertical car park served by terrifying one-car-at-a-time lifts. Then relax by playing boules on Britain's only official inner-city pétanque piste in the centre of the little, mini-sized square.

DOPING THE POISSONS D'AVRIL

It's not just the big commercial companies which see the marketing potential in April Fool's. Campaigning groups and ethical good causes have latched on too. An imaginative example was the 'tournament of sleeping fish' announced in the US six years ago. This was the brainchild of the campaigning group People for the Ethical Treatment of Animals, a serious outfit which no one ever suspected of having an urge to play practical jokes. But in 2000 they did just that, showing an appealing sense of humour and getting precious publicity by sabotaging the annual fishing tournament in Lake Palestine, Texas. Organisers were told that the lake would be massively dosed with tranquillisers which meant that nothing would bite. 'The fish will be napping not nibbling,' said PETA, as wildlife rangers and chemists were dispatched by alarmed authorities. The Feds should have done their maths. To make the trick work, the 25,500-acre reservoir would have needed more sleeping tablets than could be carried by three large sea-going oil tankers.

TO BUY OR NOT TO BUY?

A final little grin from the commercial world: in 2000 the website The Motley Fool which in spite of its name is well respected for reliable financial info risked its reputation with an April spoof. Mind you, it was so outlandish that only the very innocent would have been had. The site exclusively revealed that a secret exhumation had been held by historians in Stratford-upon-Avon, to find out more about Shakespeare. Maybe they were after his DNA. What they unexpectedly discovered was that the wise old bird had been buried along with his investment portfolio (was there a Tudor and Stuart stock exchange? No) and this was now worth some $18.7 million. The Bard's literary genius had extended to sound investment nous; his original dabble in a company called Horses Incorporated had matured through takeovers into a major holding in the Ford Motor Co.

FAMOUS FOOLERS

You've read about Horace and Virginia of *Dreadnought* fame; here are some more of their like-minded sort.

☺ **Paul Jordan Smith** wrote novels in Los Angeles in the 1920s and between times dabbled in art. He considered the Cubists, Vorticists and assorted other Ists a bit pretentious and mocked them by creating a school of his own. The Disumbrationists burst on the

world with a vivid if rather blurry painting of a South Sea islander
with a banana on her head. This was allegedly done by the Russian
artist Pavel Jerdanowitch who was of course Smith. Something of a
classical scholar, he invented the word Disumbrationist as a
weighty-sounding concept with linguistic references to emerging
from shade and refusing to take umbrage. Well aware that foreign =
intellectual in American eyes, he plastered back his hair, sunk in
his cheeks and took a photo of himself as Pavel. He submitted this
with some highfalutin nonsense about the banana woman
shattering the bonds of conventional womanhood, calling it
Exaltation. The painting was an immediate success. Smith teased
Californians further with a compilation of eyeballs and squiggles
called *Illumination* which also went down a storm. He then exposed
himself in the *LA Times* in a piece which ticked off all the Ist-
followers for their poor taste. The Disumbrationist collection is
inevitably small but black-and-white prints can be seen online of
Exaltation and *Illumination* as well as *Aspiration*, *Adoration* and *Gin-ation*,
the latter described by Pavel/Smith as a homily on the havoc
wreaked by gin in Hollywood and 'the most powerful of my works'.

☺ **Hugh Troy** was another artist with a penchant for practical jokes
although everyone who has tried to follow his tracks has ended up
in a complete muddle of truth and myth. Born in 1906, he is
supposed to have driven his family mad with pranks until they sent
him to Cornell University. There he used one of those gruesome
rhino's foot wastepaper baskets to make tracks through the snow to
the campus's reservoir Beebee Lake. Everyone thought that a zoo
animal had escaped and drowned, polluting the water which some
of the brightest young minds in the US then refused to drink. On
graduation he got a job as an illustrator in New York where he
pioneered the well-known roadworks prank: getting one group of
friends to dress up as road menders and start pick-axing, then
telling them that another group was going to come along dressed as
police, then phoning the real police . . . He also bought a bench
which he placed in Central Park and then apparently 'stole',
courting arrest which duly happened, but then showing the NYPD

his genuine receipt from the bench shop. All very studenty, but Troy went up a notch when he guyed the 1935 Van Gogh exhibition at the Museum of Modern Art by adding a fake ear made of old beef as an exhibit, labelling it as the actual one which the painter had notoriously cut off. Attendance rose, upon which Troy considered, a little haughtily, that the public was more interested in sensation, blood and gore than in Impressionist art. He got his comeuppance by spending the Second World War in a tedious administrative desk job, although he enlivened this with a fake but successful memo to fellow officers requiring them to keep a weekly register of the number of flies trapped on sticky paper rolls during the hot summer months.

☺ **Alan Abel** featured at the very start of my researches when the first index card in the catalogue of Manchester Central Library was for his *Journal of the Society for Indecency to Naked Animals*. Months later, I had finally extricated most of the twists and turns of this incorrigible fooler's long life, most of them designed to show up the media's gullibility. Abel's animal prank started in San Francisco in 1962 when a haze of pot smoke was joining the fog of the Bay Area and moral deterioration was a hot issue. In such circumstances, a bespectacled, somewhat chubby businessman in a suit seemed an entirely plausible crusader. Abel suggested that naked animals from pet poodles to bulls in the fields outside the city were inspiring juvenile delinquency and sexual crime. He offered a range of paper patterns for undergarments to fit any type of creature, including gartered stockings for goats and literally feline catsuits. Reporters wrote this all down unquestioningly and a national tour by SINA was a great success. It attracted the attention of a multi-millionaire in Florida, Maxwell Sackheim, who was let in on the secret and thenceforward bankrolled a whole series of Abel stunts. Some were linked to 1 April, others not, but alas the culmination of the series never got off the ground. Sackheim died just as Abel was completing his plans to take a fake Loch Ness monster to Scotland, and the spoofster was left with a 30-foot-long concoction of sea-green-painted plastic and chicken wire.

☺ **Revd Toby Forward** deserves a hand for having an excellent genuine name which may have inspired his solitary but inspired go at fooling. As an Anglican vicar he had promised to uphold the truth, but he may have felt that there were higher principles involved in 1987 when he answered a publisher's call for new writing. The feminist imprint Virago had asked for work in particular by teenagers and women from ethnic minority backgrounds, because they were seriously under-represented in print. Revd Forward put forward a lively collection of short stories by one Rahila Khan. She was too shy, he explained, to take the initiative with the publishers herself. Virago didn't check and if there is something especially distinctive about a youthful or minority voice, Toby had mastered it. For he was himself Rahila, albeit a white, middle-class and middle-aged man. Virago withdrew as many of the 10,000 imprint as it could find but Revd Forward's writing career went forward. He published a second well-received collection of stories set among British Asians in his own name plus a string of other books and is now a canon at Liverpool Cathedral and in charge of its contribution to next year's European Capital of Culture celebrations.

☺ **Clint Luciano Rees-Bunce** doesn't exist, needless to say, but has been a sterling alter ego for the British journalist Victor Lewis-Smith who specialises in getting up people's noses. Appropriately Sir Clint was created when the drummer in a band run by Lewis-Smith developed a nasal polyp and needed cheering up during an uncomfortable month in hospital. Reese-Bunce began life as a clergyman whose letters to local newspapers sowed confusion and in one case started a police inquiry but progressed to become a papal nuncio, film producer and fake entry in many pompous social directories, usually coming just above the former editor of *The Times*, William Rees-Mogg. He regressed briefly into a 15-year-old girl who conducted a titillating correspondence with a sausage company and then gatecrashed a TV discussion as a crusading gynaecologist dressed in a Batman outfit. His fake phone calls deluded many victims from the art critic Brian Sewell, who found himself talking

gibberish to someone with a voice even classier and more
strangulated than his own, to the hapless presenter of a local radio
gardening programme. This man took a call from a car driver who
wanted advice about a wilting cactus growing on the windscreen of
his Ford Capri. There was then a terrible smash, the sound of
breaking glass and silence. Shortly afterwards, a supposed paramedic
came on the line saying 'we've got a dead-on-arrival and his
carphone is connected to your number'. Outing himself in the
Sunday Correspondent in 1990, Lewis-Smith announced Rees-Bunce's
demise to widespread relief, on the grounds that his targets such as
daytime TV were so abysmal that they were no longer a challenge for
self-respecting foolers.

☺ **Manda Elizalde** seemed when I first lighted on her to be that rare
thing, a woman who was an obsessive fooler, but no; Manda was a
diminutive for Manuel and Mr Elizalde was a Philippines multi-
millionaire in cahoots with the country's President Marcos.
Together they hatched the idea of an undiscovered Stone Age tribe
living in remote seclusion in the jungle. Photographed in all their
prelapsarian innocence and beauty by *National Geographic*, they were
then offered the generous protection of Marcos in 1971, a major
Brownie point for a dodgy regime which needed all the good
publicity it could get. Come the day when Marcos was driven from
power, leaving behind that notorious mountain of his wife Imelda's
fashion shoes, the 'Tasaday' tribe turned out to be fakes. A couple
of them swapped their leaf skirts for jeans and blew the gaff on a
wholesale deception in which ordinary 20th-century local farmers
had been bribed to pretend to be primitive forest people for
Marcos and Elizalde's plot. So many journalists were hoaxed, and
in professional terms badly damaged, that attempts have been made
sporadically to suggest that some at least of the romantic story was
true. The kindest theory is that there was a poverty-stricken and
marginalised community, but it didn't have to wear leaf skirts.

9

Netwits and Blogfools

A lie can travel halfway round while the truth is putting on its shoes.

MARK TWAIN (ATTRIB.)

S ECOND ONLY TO GOOGLE, ONE OF THE BEST SITES ON THE INTERNET IS WIKIPEDIA, THE 'HOME-MADE' ENCYCLO- PEDIA WHICH DRAWS ON THE WIT AND WISDOM OF ANYONE WHO CARES TO LOG ON. The vast majority of its information is fascinating and accurate, but it also has that playful side which is the trademark of the online world. The word 'wiki' is an internet term (derived from a Hawaiian word) for a website which users can add to, remove from and otherwise edit. On Wikipedia you can write your entry and swell with pride as it goes out to the unseen millions. Then wince as someone who knows you makes additions and amendments. And so it goes on.

Wikipedia was the brainchild of Jimmy Donal 'Jimbo' Wales, whose father like Phineas Barnum's ran a grocery store, albeit in Alabama rather than New England. Wales also shares the great show-man's imagination and zeal, but there the comparison ends. Although his vast database is vulnerable to charlatans its aim is a noble one. In Wales's own words: 'Imagine a world in which every single person on

the planet is given free access to the sum of all human knowledge.'
Wow.

Imagine too, though, what an obvious target such an enterprise is
for April Foolers. Wales and his team make things so accessible that
the founder's own biography on Wikipedia incorporates claims and
counterclaims. Yes, it duly notes that he is the first entry in the
Scientists and Thinkers section of *Time* magazine's most recent (May
2006) list of the 100 most influential people in the world. But
allegations that he wrote a co-founder out of Wikipedia's history and
downplayed the sex content of one of his earlier, youthful internet
enterprises are also posted (along with his response). Think what
opportunities Horace de Vere Cole would have seen in all this.

He didn't live to see it, but let Wikipedia tell you in its own words
what Cole's April Fooling successors have got up to. The website
updates itself with remarkable speed and April the first was hardly
under way in 2005 before it was telling its millions of users: 'Today
Wikipedia, the free encyclopedia that anyone with access to the
Internet can edit, was the victim of an onslaught of practical jokes, as
April Fool's Day kicked in in various timezones around the world, at
least those parts which follow the Gregorian calendar. It is believed
that Wikipedia contributors were kept busy tidying up and removing
prank articles and changes made by other Wikipedia contributors, and
were expecting to be cleaning up the aftermath for days afterwards.'

Jimbo's own page on the encyclopedia was one of the targets. It
suddenly disappeared and then reappeared in Spanish. But the most
dramatic announcement was that Wikipedia had been taken over by
the *Encyclopædia Britannica*. Reactions were included from world figures
from President George W. Bush, who gave a trademark incoherent
comment, to Osama bin Laden who issued a fatwa against everyone
involved in the deal. The further readers got into the story, the more
their credulity was tested, although there was one whopping clue early
on. The most obvious initial change was apparently going to be the
imposition of the *Britannica*'s 'æ' ligature which Wikipedia had so
crudely dropped in its own title. The new Wikipædia was, for
instance, going to require its submissions in Ænglish.

Some of the dozens of other Wiki-fools were conventional; one contributor spent a long time dreaming up an 'Armoured Combat Deep Fryer', a tank converted into a sort of mobile steak and chips pan 'capable of preparing the main course of a meal, under combat conditions, for 150 soldiers'. He then designed and wrote a page for it on the encyclopedia, as part of the main entry on the genuine tank from which it was supposedly modified. He was upset when the site's techie staff tracked this down and removed it after only 20 minutes. That was against the whole point of Wikipedia, the spoofer complained in the familiar, free-spirit tone of the site's fans. Why, the decision hadn't even been through 'the Speedy Deletion Procedure' which allows brief discussion by users before false, unpleasant or otherwise dubious entries get the chop. It was too late for change, but he was given space for his plea: 'It's important to have a sense of humor and rather than trying to squash the April Fool's jokes, perhaps we should find a way to work together. How about a template that is available to mark an article as an April Fool's joke or another template that helps track changes to articles done in the name of April Fool's?'

That is what eventually happened although not through his effort. The *Britannica* April Fool is still on the site but under a large purple banner which says: 'This page is kept because it contains material which is considered **humorous**'. The bold type is Wikipedia's and for anyone who still hasn't got the point, the message goes on to warn that none of the information should be used for research, except into Wikipedia itself. An April Fool with its sting drawn, therefore; but a specimen worth preserving, especially online. The web is particularly strong in Fools fans who are less interested in catching out (or being caught out by) a spoof than in enjoying the cleverness and artifice which go into the best, or at least most complex, pranks. April Nerds? April Anoraks? Yes but don't be too critical. After all, you've bought or borrowed (but I hope not stolen) this book.

The attitude of these April Fool fans is evident, too, in the various technical tricks which were the other part of the onslaught on Wikipedia. They probably outnumbered the traditional 'make up a story' April Fool's, although I've found no record of anyone counting. Deletion notices were changed to termination tags, with pictures of the film character the Terminator. The deletion discussion page was adjusted to make it pop up as the whole Wikipedia site's home page. Article navigation tags, which enable users to link quickly between one piece and other related ones, were adjusted from outside. The category 'History', for example, was replaced by 'Time Travel'. A long-standing grouse about the Votes for Deletion page saw a picture of a kitchen toaster inserted with the caption: 'Votes for Deletion was first hosted on this BSD powered toaster. When that broke down, they had to use solar panels. Hence the reason the page loads so slowly.'

Wikipedia dealt with the bombardment efficiently but – interestingly for the internet's effect on April Fool's – staff had to stay on the alert for two days rather than one. Pranksters online have twice as long to play around as their earthbound predecessors, as the encyclopedia itself ruefully pointed out. 'Being accessible worldwide (by people who can afford Internet access) in all timezones, April Fool's Day lasts for more than 24 hours here.' The old limitation of getting your joke done in the morning of April the first, or else you are the April Fool, has been killed by information technology. Online it's April Fool's *Days*, not Day.

Not all the spoofs were deleted. What the site called 'tacit community consensus' left some of the more harmless ones such as Time Travel in place for users to enjoy, just as the *Britannica* spoof survives beneath its purple health warning. But the debate continues because just as some of *Panorama*'s spaghetti viewers had issues about trust, so the pure wikireaders want a basic sense of good order. One of them posted a cry for help: 'This is getting out of hand. Sneak vandalism everywhere, and it seems like every wikiuser feels they should have their own April Fool's prank somewhere. I'm thinking maybe the best joke would be to let Wikipedia not be editable on April Fool's Day. Use the day to reindex tablebases or whatever it is that a day off can be used constructively to do. Wikipedia should be correct all the year. God knows how long all this misinformation will live on on forgotten pages around the net.'

Quite so. Like the invented story of the Emperor Constantine and Jester Kugel, which survives unchallenged on many sites, or a clutch of other tall stories about the internet itself. No sooner had the World Wide Web begun to develop from an inter-university system and a military adaption of it, than the spoofers got going. As early as 1978 an April Fooler advertised a system called 'Randomly Lose' which supposedly controlled early online computers' tendency to crash or fail to save data. But the first really big hoax was in 1984, an appropriately Orwellian year to tease Big Brother which is what this one did. A message was posted on the premier online forum of the day, the Usenet bulletin board, from Konstantin Chernenko, the last pre-glasnost general secretary of the Soviet Union.

'Well, today, 840401, this is at last the Socialist Union of Soviet Republics joining the Usenet network and saying hello to everyone,' it started cheerily. Readers all over the web, which was tiny by today's standards and largely in the United States, jumped out of their chairs. The message went on to say that the USSR saw the new technology as a 'means of having an open discussion forum with the American and European people'. Reverting to a more authentically Kremlin tone, it acknowledged that many in the West would hold anti-Russian opinions, but this was simply because they 'have been misguided by their leaders, especially the American administration, which is seeking for war and the domination of the world'.

The techie stuff all looked convincing. The IT codes were correct and the Soviet leader was using the email address chernenko@kremvax.UUCP – krem for Kremlin, vax being the acronym at the time for Virtual Address eXtension (as well as an American brand of vacuum cleaners which fought a protracted copyright battle with the computer people), and UUCP a computer connection code which looked fortuitously like a Cyrillic version of USSR. The message aped the chatty style which emails were beginning to develop in this period of their infancy. It ended convivially: 'And now, let's open a flask of vodka and have a drink on our entry to this network. So: NA ZDAROVJE! - Cheers! There was a flood of replies, great excitement across the online world and even, allegedly, a serious discussion at the Pentagon about how to deal with this latest 'Red problem'. I say 'allegedly' because my only source for that is the man who was the real 'Konstantin Chernenko' and creator of kremvax: an extremely clever systems operator in the Netherlands who was central to the building of Europe's first version of the internet.

His name was Piet Beertema, 41 at the time of the hoax and a keen ballroom dancer and organist outside his otherwise all-consuming interest in computers. He became central technical manager of what was to become EUnet and also pioneered the Dutch branch which in turn developed into NLnet and then UUNet Nederland. In between coping with the legal battles, codes and number-crunching, he found time to write satirical poems about the problems he encountered online.

Piet broke cover in 1984 after a fortnight of frenzied international computer activity, which saw several institutions raise concerns about the cost of communicating with kremvax. In those days, you had to dial up on slow phone connections and it wasn't cheap. Piet must also have been getting tired of emptying his inbox to which all the communications to Mr Chernenko were redirected. He posted a message on Usenet on 15 April headed 'The Mystery Unravelled'. It thanked all his 'netpals' who had replied, especially those who spotted his clues which included mentioning the April 1st date twice in the text. And it ruefully added 'Sorry for those who took this April Fool so bloody seriously. I got serious letters more than three pages long.'

Actually a lot of the correspondents sussed that they were dealing with a joker, some praising his or her cleverness, others deploring 'bad form'. But there were also redneck ripostes, telling the Soviet leader where to go sometimes with four-letter words; and other rather sweet replies which looked forward to reconciliatory post-Cold War chats. A Canadian, for instance, emailed reassuringly that Chernenko would find Canadian politics 'much less strident' than American ones, a claim borne out by the tone of many of the American messages.

Several people assumed that the hoaxer would be sacked, but Beertema went from strength to strength, even ending up to his surprise in 1999 with the award of Knight of the Order of the Netherlands Lion, a Dutch royal decoration for exceptional merit or as he describes it on his website 'for doing apparently useful things'. Looking back at the hoax now, he says: 'Nothing in particular prompted it. It was just one of those silly ideas that I come up with now and then. Except that this one got stuck in my mind. And while it was stuck, I suddenly recalled the book by the Soviet dissident Andrej Amalrik, *Will the Soviet Union survive until 1984?* Bingo! The time was right to prove it did, and I had the means to hand.' The Soviet Union only just made it, collapsing in 1991, and the real Konstantin Chernenko never got to know the joys of global emailing. He died in 1985 and was succeeded by the man who brought about the political breakthrough, Mikhail Gorbachev. That brought a nice envoi to Piet's prank. When the new Russia started connecting online in earnest in 1991, one of the first domain names to be registered by the country's democratic politicians was kremvax.demos.su.

So Piet set things rolling. On his website he mourns the way that spam became a bad fairy of the breakthroughs in IT communication which he and others pioneered. But he was happy to see spoofs multiply in a similar way and – to an extent which even the best tricks on TV could not match – reach multi-million audiences worldwide. One of the neatest was actually a reworking of an old telephone joke, but it worked. Very large numbers of users were persuaded on April Fool's Day 1997 that the whole internet was going to be closed for 24 hours for spring cleaning.

The phone version of this trick was mechanically based. Subscribers were rung by pranksters pretending to be the local telephone exchange who asked them to put plastic bags over their receivers to catch any dust which might be blown out during the annual cleaning of local phone lines, which was about to take place in their area. On the net, the message took an appropriately IT line, explaining that discarded data and 'electronic flotsam and jetsam' needed to be cleared up so that the millions of connections could operate efficiently and not be slowed down. It appeared to come from the mighty Massachusetts Institute of Technology, signed by a Kim Dereksen of the Interconnected Network Maintenance Staff Main Branch and using all the appropriate email protocols and codes.

Mr (or it may have been Ms) Dereksen explained that for the next 24 hours 'five very powerful Japanese built multi-lingual internet-crawling robots (Toshiba ML-2274) situated around the world will search the internet and delete any data that they find'. So far, so undemanding. But as with the telephone plastic bags, internet users needed to do their bit. All internet connections should be closed and computer terminals shut down, said Dereksen, still in convincingly matter-of-fact language. And then came the credibility-strainers. The last two instructions were: Avoid placing operating microwave ovens or toasters near your computer modem. And avoid wearing nylon (or other dielectric fibre) undergarments because of the possibility of electrical discharge.

If you didn't smell a rat by then, you were a sucker. But it was too late for many who had already obediently switched their computers off. The trick even worked in later years when it reappeared signed by a sysop, or systems operator, called Yuben T. Ricked. As for the original, I have fed 'Kim Dereksen' and the name of the MIT department into anagram programs without success. Details such as dielectric fibres and the Toshiba ML series do exist. The Fool was very well concealed with only sophisticated clues such as the sinister phrase 'As many of you will know' (an echo of the *Panorama* spaghetti harvest, and Richard Dimbleby's assertion that 'Many of you, I am sure, will have seen pictures of vast spaghetti plantations in the Po Valley'). The notion of internet cleaning was a con whose creators really wanted it to work.

The mysterious Dereksen, a name unknown at MIT, had actually sent out a more modest version of the spoof the previous year, which largely escaped notice because it was emailed at the end of February rather than on April Fool's Day. After the second strike in 1997, he or she spawned many imitators. New users were joining the internet all the time and many of the older ones had a vague notion of the web as a physical construct which would require dusting and probably nuts and bolts. Being the age I am, I sympathise and I'm sure that I would have been caught by another online April Fool which targeted this naive group.

In April 1994 the American magazine *PC Computing* ran a news piece revealing that a bill was about to go through Congress making it illegal to use the internet when drunk. Discussion of sexual matters online would also be forbidden, which would close down a very large section of today's web. The FBI was preparing to deploy agents to tap the phones of known alcohol abusers and the bill was expected to get an easy passage because few politicians would want to appear as public defenders of drunkenness or online sex. As news of the article spread, big guns such as Senator Edward Kennedy were rumoured to be behind the legislation and there was quite a stir – letters, calls and emails to Capitol Hill and official denial from Kennedy whose past involvement in the tragic death of Mary Jo Kopechne, a controversy involving allegations of drunk driving and sex, made him a natural butt for such pranks. Only gradually did realisation spread about the significance of the bill's number, 040194, and the name of a congressional contact who could supply further details: Lirpa Sloof.

The drink-driving joke was partly based on the layman's term for the net of 'Information Superhighway' which was common at the time. Indeed the article discussed whether Congress members had introduced the law on the grounds that it was dangerous to be drunk on the highway 'no matter what kind of highway it is'. Given the amount of scamming and fraud that happens online nowadays, perhaps they had a point. And it was only two years before Congress introduced a genuine Communications Decency Bill which tried rather clumsily to outlaw indecency on the internet but fell foul of the First Amendment on free speech at the Supreme Court.

At the opposite end of the spectrum from innocents deluded about spring cleaning and drink-driving online, the web community has developed an enormous array of technical April Fool's which the outsider may find hard to untangle. On a typical website, www.2meta.com/april fools/, a poll of users' favourite pranks gives an overwhelming vote for best-ever April Fool on the internet to the '1994 JPEG virus alert', a piece of fictitious technobabble which convinced many expert users that picture files could carry secret viruses when transmitted online. As with the drink-driving spoof and Congress's genuine attempts to regulate the web, the joke had connections with reality. You can read for many hours online about later, genuine alerts from Microsoft and others about similar-sounding perils. But I warn you that it is hard work. More relaxing are the many variants on the computer cupholder April Fool, most recently sprung by a Polish website in 2004. Click on this link, it said, and you will get a handy place to put coffee or other drinks which won't then spill onto your keyboard and ruin it. Click – and whirr, out slides your CD drive (for non-computer folk, a plastic tray with a cup-shaped hole in the middle). Almost as funny as the joke are the internet discussion threads of geeks discussing whether or not to click the link, and when they do, debating what the message in Polish on their screen means. It says: Gotcha.

It's a short step from these techno-Fools to the endless universe of the bloggers, or blogosphere, which can be every bit as as tedious as it sounds. There are some great writers out there but web loggers, or online diarists equipped with clever extras of the internet such as hyperlinks to other sites and interaction with readers, are notoriously prone to verbal diarrhoea. Their April Fool's japes are innumerable but much less varied in content than you might imagine. Googling at random, I lit immediately on a blog whose prank proved to be stereo-typical. Its author had created a link for the day marked simply UnderageNudeGirl which 'a ton of men and boys clicked on SO fast'. It took them, naturally, to the even shorter message 'April Fool!' and a head and shoulders photo of the bearded blogger himself, wearing nothing but a triumphant grin.

If this book isn't enough for you, you can navigate for the rest of your life, and then some, round the blogosphere's April Fool's jokes. And if the actual japes themselves are not usually rewarding, the bloggers are so internet-minded that they can lead you to some really excellent ones which you might never find on your own. Piet Beertema made the point to me that online pranks often have a smaller audience these days than in the primitive world of 1984. 'The time then was perfect for my April Fool,' he said. 'There was only a very, very limited number of main newsgroups or bulletin boards so an article reached virtually everyone reading newsgroups – and that was already a lot of people. Nowadays it would be impossible to carry out a joke like kremvax because there's no longer such a thing as "main newsgroups"; there are half a zillion of them.'

Many a witty flower is therefore doomed to blush unseen. Except when the blogosphere latches on to it and spreads the word. So thanks to the UnderageNudeGirl blogger for directing me to my favourite online April Fool: the tiny aliens who dropped in on the United

States' top-secret 'Area 51' experimental base on April the first last year and had a barbecue.

Area 51 is a 60-square-mile, sealed-off chunk of Nevada where all sorts of classified things go on, supposedly involving experimental planes and rockets. It has a large US Air Force base which goes under a string of other nicknames, Dreamland, The Box, Paradise Ranch, and has been the focus for countless spooky rumours. Genuine history includes the testing of the notorious U2 high-level spying plane and the evacuation of the base in 1957 when it was sprayed with fallout from nearby nuclear bomb tests. The US government neither denies nor confirms its existence but 'lethal force' is authorised against anyone who trespasses across its perimeter.

The Area has naturally become an icon for conspiracy theorists and UFO buffs, as well as a favourite wallpaper for computer games. It forms part of the plot in the hit game *Tomb Raider III* and the whole of it in a series of novels and a rock musical. Papers have been written on the base's alleged 'magic' airstrip called the Cheshire, because it only appears when water is sprayed on its camouflage and then vanishes soon afterwards like the cat in Lewis Carroll's *Alice's Adventures in Wonderland*. Those who believe that the Americans never went to the moon are convinced that the landings were simulated in the area's cratered and lunar-looking landscape. Above all, Area 51 is believed to be much visited by aliens.

All good fun. But in the last five years, satellite photographs have allowed the rest of the world to spy on the spooks, and that is where the April Fool was hatched. Google has a marvellous program called Google Earth, which allows you to home in on anywhere on the planet, zooming in on the satellite data until you see your own car parked outside your own home. On April the first last year, several bloggers decided to give Area 51 a peep. Scanning the vast arid area, they gradually homed in on the air force base and checked out the hangars and aprons dotted with parked military jets. Hang on, what was that? Scoping up the magnification, they found a small dot next to what looks like an F-15 fighter.

Moving to maximum zoom, they discovered a beautifully mocked-up flying saucer with two turquoise aliens, one cleaning the craft's windscreen while the other prodded burgers on a barbie. Word spread, prompted by a gentle hint about Area 51 which Google Earth put on its community forum. It wasn't long before the servers which handled the internet traffic to the site got perilously close to overload. Out of respect for the tradition about not keeping April Fool's going beyond the morning, or at least the day, Google removed its aliens on April the second. But you can still check them out on websites. Or you might prefer to enjoy tributes down here on Earth. Next time you're in Hamburg, bob in to see the world's largest model railway layout, whose American section includes not only Area 51 but a team of tiny extraterrestrials playing basketball with base personnel.

CLICK FOR A FOOL

WIRELESS EVERYTHING

The fantastic pace of change on the internet and in information technology more widely has made almost anything credible when new developments are announced. This accounts for the initial delight at 130 major companies which were sent a detailed package in April 1999 about 'total home remote electricity'. Wireless computers and the whole wi-fi breakthrough were hot news and this seemed the next logical development. Electricity itself could be beamed anywhere in an ordinary domestic house. An 'aura' of high-voltage but safe power would envelope your home, allowing any electrical appliance to be used anywhere. 'Did you ever imagine making toast on your roof?' asked one of the accompanying flyers, which should have alerted the hard-bitten execs. But around 30 of them rang the number given for more information. April Fool! replied the giggling staff at Hoffman York, the advertising agency which devised the spoof.

MEANWHILE ELSEWHERE IN THE MARKET . . .

Here's one from the same year, 1999, that went wrong, because it was just too convincingly done. While those company execs were getting excited about wireless electricity, an announcement appeared on the news service Business Wire about incredibly powerful new data-carriers on what was called the 'Next Generation Internet'. Known as nodes, each of these was extremely powerful and with enormous capacity. But because there were going to be 50 million of them, punters could buy one for just 100 dollars. A company called Webnode had been set up to sell them, with every hope that they would soar in value because of the huge amount of traffic on the web. The more use of a node, the more it would be worth and node-owners would also be able to charge a sort of toll to users. It was just too node to be true but vast numbers fell for it, causing masses of unnecessary emailing, grief and embarrassment for Business Wire. The agency eventually started a damages action for fraud, breach of contract, defamation, and conspiracy which meant that spoofers have treated it warily ever since.

BEWARE, BEWARE OF POLO FLAIR

Uh-oh. How could anyone get away with a new invention-based company called Polo Flair? The *Straits Times* in Singapore did in 1999 with a report that a nerdy local teenager had created a small, cheap computer program which guaranteed to kill off the 'Year 2000' computer bug which was causing great consternation at the time. All the big players in the online world were wrestling with the problem – the possibility that computer clocks would fail to understand the concept of a new millennium and would reset everything, plunging all computer-controlled systems into chaos. And now this Chinese lad had sorted out a solution in less than half an hour while doing his algebra homework. His family were supposed to be looking for financial partners and talking about annual takings of £40 million but the boy proved terminally elusive. It was after all April the first, as other news media and would-be investors gradually sussed.

MIND GAMES

It sounded ludicrous but the magazine *Red Herring* did it very well: an announcement that a new technology (yes, yet another) had finally made telepathic emails possible. Ha ha. But the article convincingly followed the magazine's reporter to the offices of Tidal Wave Communications, run by a Mr Yuri Maldini from Estonia, whose name produces nothing sinister when fed into anagram programs. Maldini had all sorts of down-to-earth details about how he had helped the US Army during the first Gulf War where he learned extraordinary secrets from encrypting online messages into code. But the clincher came when *Red Herring*'s reporter asked how big the market would be, and Maldini stared silently out of his office window. The genius then turned back and said: 'I just sent you a telepathic email with my answer.' When the journalist got back to *Red Herring*'s office, the email was in his inbox. It said: 'It's going to be huge.' That pay-off convinced an impressive number of readers who admitted to *Red Herring* that it had them fooled.

MUMMY I WANT TO GO

The brand name iPod has rapidly become a familiar term but it wasn't until April last year that anyone had heard of the iPood. The Seattle Podcasting Network reported on April the first that a Danish company called Tanterflügn had invented this 'unique, interactive toilet training device for toddlers'. Available in playful colours, the device used a Bluetooth connection to link a gauge on the infant's tummy to an adapted iPod which then started using 'gentle words of encouragement recorded by some of today's most popular fictional characters'. Success on the potty was then rewarded by snippets of audio from Elmo giggling to Barney the Dinosaur roaring 'You're a sooper-dee-dooper pooper!' The spokesman for Tanterflügn was predictably called Tørd.

SOMETHING IN THE WATER

A Californian student called Eric Lechner started a long trail of havoc in April 1990 when he sent out an email which sounded the alarm about foam cups used for coffee and other hot drinks. The message described how research showed that their production involved the use of dihydrogen monoxide, a material 'used as an industrial solvent and coolant'. It was a time of even more nerves than usual about chemicals, with controversy burgeoning about genetically modified crops and other Frankensteiny products of the labs. There were many victims of Lechner's initiative, most notably the local council of Aliso

Viejo, also in California, which called a vote on whether to ban foam cups from any event organised by the city. This was called off when the city manager, David J. Norman, admitted that one of his paralegal staff had fallen down on their research. Dihydrogen monoxide, better known as H_2O, is water.

PI IN THE SKY

A journalist called April Holiday ought to attract immediate suspicion, but the fictional young lady's exclusive in 1998 caused impressively lasting havoc. Tagged as an Associated Press reporter, she was invented by pranksters at the normally staid newsletter of New Mexicans for Science and Reason in 1998. To parody their state's toying with Creationism in schools as an alternative to evolution, the group's president Dave Thomas wrote April's piece under the headline 'Alabama lays siege to Pi'. It revealed that the neighbouring state was planning to make life easier for school students by reducing the mathematical constant's value from the tricky 3.14159 (and so on) to a round 3. Thomas admitted the hoax immediately after the midday deadline and it served his purpose of getting newspaper headlines and airtime for the evolution debate. But other hoaxers used the internet to spread the story all over the world and Alabama's legislature had a long, weary time fielding outraged scholarly calls.

INTERACTIVE BUGS

University security teams are often rather po-faced individuals, saddled with serious jobs while youthful irresponsibility waxes blithely around them. Not so at Queen's University at Kingston in the Canadian province of Ontario whose security department has a fine reputation for April jests. This was enhanced in 2003 when they put out an interactive fool with the initially credible headline 'Alert: Computer bugs reported across campus'. The message below said that students had contacted security early in the morning (sounds an unlikely time for student activity but still) to say that they had unusual problems with their computers. A security check had revealed that the intranet was indeed crawling with bugs. 'Not a virus,' said a spokesman. 'Real bugs. Loads of them. From the campus sewers.' Pest controllers were on the way, but meanwhile it had been discovered that the bugs were sensitive to computer mouse movements which should be used in the short term to chase them off screens. You have to log on to experience the real cleverness of the joke – www.queensu.ca/security/archive/themes/april1/2003/april1.html. If you can't, I can only tell you that hideously realistic bugs do appear and it's great fun chasing them away with the mouse. Final touch: a click on a hyperlink marked 'For more information and preventive measures' takes you to a search engine's history of April Fool's.

TEN TERRIBLE TRICKS

☺ **Glue** together the sheets of the morning newspaper

☺ **Place** a plastic bowl of water on top of a slightly open door

☺ **Put** the clocks an hour forward

☺ **Repeatedly** pat or 'dust' a friend's back and get others to do the same, to induce dandruff paranoia

☺ **Write** letter from your employer to yourself announcing promotion and move to Newfoundland with details of children's schooling package etc and open in presence of your partner

☺ **Sew** up trouser fly

☺ **Place** clingfilm over the lavatory on top of bowl but below seat. Avoid creases.

☺ **Check out** some of the truly horrible prank computer programs available on the net; one appears to wipe all your files, complete with realistic noises from the hard drive

☺ **Pour** tea (Earl Grey has a nice scent) into a steam iron

☺ **Replace** loved one's shampoo with syrup

10

Weird But True

Life is an abnormal business.
EUGENE IONESCO, *RHINOCEROS*, ACT II

S OME YEARS AGO I WENT AS A JOURNALIST ON AN INSECT-COLLECTING EXPEDITION TO INDONESIA. The extraordinary methods used by the scientists to trap their prey have stayed with me ever since – gas puffed into the forest canopy, beetle-dungeons hidden under rotting wood and a mixture of sweet rum and sticky treacle painted onto tree trunks to intoxicate moths. But my favourite was a mega-net mounted on a Land Rover which then bounced about in the dark, headlights blazing, to sweep up more prey. I recognised its airborne relation at once when I turned to the *Daily Telegraph* on 1 April 1993 and found much of page five devoted to 'The world's first and finest flying moth-collecting machine'.

Nothing daft about that, I thought, remembering the antics of my entomologists on Sulawesi island who would have jumped at the chance to swoop above the Dumoga-Bone forest in the *Telegraph*'s microlight with its nosecone ultraviolet moth-attracting lamp, twin spotlights and special airflow speed reducer which ensured that moths were sucked into two collecting funnels at a gentle 5 mph. That wasn't how most journalists reacted however. The next day, the amazing moth machine featured in rival papers' lists of obvious April Fool's, in some cases with a scornful subtext about the dear old *Torygraph* trying on such an obvious spoof.

Except that it was real, accurate and genuine – and a fine example of how truth on April Fool's Day can often be every bit as strange as invention. The misguided reporters who assumed the story was the *Telegraph*'s hoax can hardly be blamed. None of them, I'm pretty sure, had been on a genuine moth hunt and seen the fanaticism involved. Also, in the way of many perfectly true stories, some of the cast list in the piece had slightly suspicious names: a Ms Friederike von Dewitz for example. But she existed and still does; indeed she is now quite big in the geography of sustainable tourism and global change. OK then but don't tell us that Lord Rothschild really used a gun to shoot moths out of trees in the 19th century as the piece claimed? He did, using a special weapon called powder shot which also allowed him to bring down tiny hummingbirds undamaged for subsequent taxidermy. Finally the author, the *Telegraph*'s science editor Roger Highfield, was a man whose byline had been attached to many fantastic-sounding stories about boffins' breakthroughs. But he too knew his stuff.

Another example was *The Times* front-page story on 1 April 2004 which appeared to be a blatant spoof: at the height of the Cold War the British government had agreed to ward off the Soviet threat with the help of a 'chicken-powered nuclear bomb'. Stuffier readers probably took one look at the headline and turned the page with a grump about the top people's paper wasting space on April Fool's. If so, they missed a fascinating story which had emerged from government papers released from the National Archives. This is a process which now happens every month, and there are so many files and bundles that the archivists always pick out a selection of likely headline-grabbers to help us journalists. I have done this job several times and you go down to Kew and get to see the new material at about 10 a.m. with a copy deadline of round about 4 p.m. That's very little time to make any serious attempt at your own research, unless you are a specialist who knows that a particular set of sensitive papers is due for release. So most of us are only too grateful for the archivists' preselection.

All credit, then, to the one who spotted the file on Operation Blue Peacock and took a closer look – and then realised how perfect this story would be for a Non-Fool on 1 April. The secret project was a plan to store a defence line of 10-kiloton nuclear bombs on the German border if war was considered imminent. They would have been detonated by wire in case of a Soviet invasion but if disturbed they would go off after eight seconds. This small-scale Armageddon was duly developed in 1954 by scientists in the Armament Research and Development Establishment at Fort Halstead in Kent, and they discovered a problem. The bombs were to be buried underground and it was realised that they would get so cold in winter that their mechanisms might fail. Various ploys were suggested including wrapping them in blankets and – here comes the poultry – sealing live chickens inside the bombs' casings with a supply of food and water which would last for the high-tension period which would see the bombs being put in place. The body heat of the birds was calculated to be enough to keep the temperature high enough to maintain this deadly ambush. And so, yes, there really was a plan for a British chicken-powered nuclear bomb. The Army got as far as ordering ten in 1957 and preparing a cover story that they were atomic power units for logistical troop support. But the risks and potentially devastating fallout from an accident persuaded the Ministry of Defence to cancel the whole of Blue Peacock the following year. As the spokesman for the National Archive commented when journalists rang to check if the story was made-up: 'The civil service doesn't do April Fool's.'

You might think that such 'stranger than fiction' revelations come once a decade or even less frequently. Not a bit of it. Awareness of the phenomenon goes back a long way in the media. In 1924 the Pathé film company released a one-reel short by the then hugely popular comedian Charley Chase. The 85th out of the 225 films he made, it was called *April Fool* and took place in a newspaper office whose staff – Jimmy Jump the cub reporter and his lover the editor's daughter – were finding it impossible to tell genuine news items from hoax ones. Any year since then can provide a rich crop of suspicious-sounding but real events. In 2005, for example, sceptics wrongly decided that media April Fool's included the following list of stories, all of which were actually true. The Home Secretary was asked to pardon Anne Boleyn, the second wife of King Henry VIII, for crimes of adultery, incest and witchcraft for which she was beheaded in 1536. The BBC put in an official request to interview the singer Bob Marley who had died in 1981. The tea tablet was invented in the Indian province of Assam as an alternative to teabags (which proved short-lived). Pope John Paul was thought to have died, which did not happen until the next day, while an American comedian called Mitch Hedberg was accused of faking his obituary because he had appeared on a network show only a week earlier. He couldn't have done a spoof obit as he had genuinely been dead for three days.

The difficulty of teasing out the real from the imaginary has meanwhile been compounded by the fact that some tabloid newspapers run stories which sound like April Fool's on almost every day of the year. The *Daily Express*'s extraordinary obsession with Princess Diana conspiracy theories, which vies for the front-page splash with sensational weather predictions, may well be revealed eventually as one of the longest-running spoofs of all time. The *Sun* has long been skilled in picking up 'isn't that odd?' stories from local news agencies and of course on 13 March 1986 (couldn't they have waited 19 days?) produced 'Freddie Starr Ate My Hamster' with its equally inspired strapline 'Comic put a live pet in sandwich, says beauty'. The comedian didn't of course, although he did own the 1994 Grand National winner Minnehoma, which is almost as hard to believe. The *Daily Sport* meanwhile took 'news' into regions where even the boldest April Fooler, or Max Clifford, the publicist behind the hamster spoof, might fear to tread. Who can forget 'WWII bomber found on moon'? Such mind-stretching notions need brains and the editor at the time had a classics degree from Oxford.

As if this carefree blurring of news and nonsense wasn't enough, the internet has taken things further. The search engine Google has a record of very clever April Fool's but as described in Chapter 8 it also chooses the day to launch genuinely innovative new products. The marketing strategy is to sow confusion deliberately, knowing the way that rumours form the lifeblood of online chat rooms and blogs. So was the new Gmail service announced in 2004 a spoof, with its then incredible option for web-based mail of a gigabyte of storage? No, it was real. Likewise, the following year's announcement of Google Ride

Finder, offering taxi firms and fare rates throughout the world, was also suspected as a hoax but turned out to be the genuine article.

Google's deliberate muddling caused problems for others. In 2003 two big Japanese video game companies, Squaresoft and Enix, announced a merger into a joint company called Square Enix which many people simply disbelieved. It had to be a jointly planned hoax, surely. It wasn't. Across the Pacific, an internet entrepreneur called Larry Butler burst into tears in his office at freecar.com, a new company which was about to test a business model based on people driving for free in cars plastered with advertisements. He had just read a piece in *Esquire* magazine about a new firm called Freewheelz which offered just that: a free car if you accepted ads on the outside and continuous advertising on the car radio. Mr Butler only realised that he had been a victim of the April Fool's Day smudge between real business start-ups and hoax ones when he got to the detail: applicants for Freewheelz also had to fill in a 600-question survey which included asking for your political opinions and whether you were worried about hair loss. And the first free vehicles to be offered were from a fleet of Stayfresh Tampons minivans. Also coming up were cars sponsored by DearSkin.com, which risked the considerable wrath of animal rights campaigners by plugging 'leather coats and gloves made exclusively from the hides of deer that have been culled from suburban woods'.

The *Independent* newspaper managed a cunning twist on the hybrid April Fool last year, with a double-page spread headed 'Romantic revelations: The Odd Couples', which looked at peculiar pairings among celebrity figures. Prompted by claims in a new biography of Barbra Streisand that the singer had 'romanced' Prince Charles, both at an extended 'tea date' in a Los Angeles hotel and later under the prying eyes of his staff at Highgrove, John Walsh featured six other strange bedfellows. They were inspirationally chosen: Delia Smith was said to have tried out her offal recipes on Graham Norton in his 'pre-gay' period so relentlessly that he confessed bursting out to her, after one fried intestine too many, 'Delia, I hate your guts.' Sylvia Plath had a groupie session with Chuck Berry, Condoleezza Rice and Jasper Carrott shared an interest in guitar music and appeared together in a production of *The Mikado* in Birmingham, and Ian Woosnam teamed up with Germaine Greer when he was a penniless student posing for life classes at the 'Ecoles Superieurs of Toulouse and Marseilles'.

Finally Barbara Windsor and Bamber Gascoigne were said to have met just before he was propelled to fame as the compère of BBC TV's *University Challenge*. On one memorable evening, the actress serenaded the high table of Gascoigne's old Cambridge college with 'I'm one of the nuts from Barcelona' after contributing to a seminar on urban dialect. Yes indeedy. But the make-believe was given credibility not just by the inclusion of Prince Charles and Streisand but by John Major and Edwina Currie – perhaps the most bizarre of all these mismatches, yet the only one which was unquestionably true.

It isn't surprising that many genuine business people avoid I April for announcing new initiatives; a very early example of this was when the maiden run of the Rolls-Royce in 1904 was put back to 31 March by Charles Rolls and Henry Royce to avoid pranks and practical jokes. The managers of Radio 538 in the Netherlands must have wished that they had followed the same policy when they ran a listeners' mystery trip offer on I April 2006. The instructions were to bring the necessaries for a weekend break to Rotterdam railway station and catch a special outing train organised by DJs. Wary of what sounded suspiciously like a jape, the punters stayed away in droves. Only three people turned up. The unsmiling group of army officers who overthrew the democratically elected government of Brazil on I April 1964 also lived to regret their choice of date. Their military regime creaked unhappily along for 21 years before democracy was restored, but its birth day is still known in Brazil as 'the worst April Fool's Joke ever'.

In the same way, the tsunami which followed an earthquake in the Aleutian Islands on I April 1946 is still known in Hawaii as the April Fool's Tsunami. It killed 165 people on the Pacific islands and led to the creation of the Pacific Tsunami Warning Centre three years later, largely because many had dismissed verbal and radio warnings that a wave was coming as a prank.

STRANGE   BUT   TRUE

HAIR RAISING

The North-East port of Hartlepool is always good for a superior joke, and the canard that locals hanged a monkey in the Napoleonic wars in mistake for a French spy has been dragged out countless times to prove how thick Hartlepudlians are. Which they aren't. In 1991 a hairdresser from the town made headlines in *The Times* for using basic chemistry from his knowledge of hair perms to invent a material which was resistant to the first searing flash of a nuclear explosion. By Sod's Law, this story broke on 31 March and *The Times*'s night editor had to protect it on its journey into the next day's edition by attaching a note saying: 'This report is not an April Fool.'

THE LETTERS THAT LEAKED

A Dutch student downloading music with the Limewire program last year thought he had discovered a cunningly buried April Fool. The usual material suddenly gave way to a string of emails from Queen Beatrix of the Netherlands and her son Prince Willem-Alexander. Details of the private life of the Dutch royals seemed an obscure sort of joke, but the lad passed them on to *De Telegraaf*, the biggest-circulation newspaper in the Netherlands. Journalists made initially ho-ho-ho enquiries, but no: the messages were genuine and had somehow escaped electronically from the Ministry of Defence. They weren't published but the leak was, following early gaffes by Dutch defence ministry officials which included leaving computer data in a car. The government finally quashed any lingering notions that this was a prank by saying that it was being taken 'very seriously'.

VORSPRUNG DURCH VITAMIN C

Just about everyone who read Luke Harding's exclusive in the *Guardian* on 1 April two years ago thought it was the annual April Fool. He revealed that the German football team which famously won the 1954 World Cup had been accused, a whole half-century later, of cheating. A groundsman at the Swiss stadium where the Germans beat Hungary in the final against all the odds was apparently going to tell a TV documentary that he had found several syringes in the team's dressing room; the team's doctor was quoted as saying that he had indeed given jabs, but only of vitamin C which was within the rules. Whatever the truth of all that, the allegations were not a Fool at all, but had appeared in the mass-circulation *Bild Zeitung* and were genuinely convulsing Germany. The story is a textbook example of the fine line between fiction-writing and the real, often bizarre, thing. After Germany's 3–2 victory, for instance, eight players fell ill and the doctor admitted that the needles might not have been sterilised properly by 'an old Soviet 'cooker' (or medical steriliser) which possibly failed to reach the correct temperature to kill germs.'

WATCH OUT, TRUTH ABOUT

Just to give an idea of the annual range of True Story hazards for Fool spotters, here's a shortlist from 2004. As well as the Queen of the Netherlands, you had to watch out for: a bizarre child-animal born in Nepal; Post Office 'reforms' which meant that TV licences could no longer be renewed over the counter and much-loved licence savings stamps – once imprinted with photographs of Prince Charles and Princess Anne as children – would be scrapped; the discovery of the world's hottest chilli pepper, registering 876,000 Scoville units and growing in the unlikely setting of a Dorset garden; plans for a film of *The Simpsons* and Jack Straw calling the US Secretary of State Condoleezza Rice a condom in a slip of his tongue. All were true.

PRANKSTERS IN THE PINK

April Fool's can of course be so prescient that they become true. Alternatively, their organisers may be shamed by the disappointment, when they dash raised expectations, into relenting and going ahead with their spoof plans anyway. The world of football has examples of both. A prank by the *Sun* about plans to widen goalposts to increase scoring and satisfy goal-hungry crowds and viewers has since become a matter of serious discussion. Bristol Rovers meanwhile announced on April Fool's Day 2005 that a spoof new strip, coloured pink, would be added to their blue, white and yellow kit. It was a joke but 2,000 fans demanded them and so the club produced a limited edition with £3 from each sale going to breast cancer charities. Last year's follow-up claimed that a Bath-style mineral spring had erupted under their pitch and the water would be bottled and sold. Naturally it was pink.

Collapse of Stout Party – Fools That Failed

You couldn't fool your mother on the foolingest day of your life even if you had an electrified fooling machine.

HOMER SIMPSON

*a*BOUT A HUNDRED YEARS AGO TWO OF BRITAIN'S GREATEST PHYSICISTS WERE CONDUCTING AN OPTICAL EXPERIMENT WHEN ONE OF THEM, JAMES CLERK MAXWELL, DECIDED TO PLAY AN APRIL FOOL. He made a tiny little paper man and fitted it with a concealed thread which allowed the manikin apparently to dance. Then he sneaked it under the lens. Peering at the experiment, his colleague, Lord Kelvin, agreed that Maxwell's serious observations were correct and then added: 'But Maxwell, what is the little man there for?' Maxwell urged him to have another look but got the same puzzled question from the great thinker. Abashed, he was eventually reduced to saying: 'He's there just for *fun*.'

April Fool's spoofs dance in vain in front of the world's uncomprehending Lord Kelvins, and they also face a wider problem common to all types of humour. Someone will burst out laughing at a joke which leaves others cold. Look at these two Massachusetts teenagers commenting on an internet April Fool's forum. 'That is the stupidest prank ever it sucks – Emily.' 'Same thing as Emily it is really stupid and has no point. Losers – Allison.' Which spoof were they discussing? The *Panorama* spaghetti harvest, which comes in most Top Tens and which I rate the best April Fool ever. Maybe you had to be there.

But if one woman's sidesplitter is another man's total dud, there are plenty of more technical reasons why April Fool's can go wrong. For a start, they can simply be too clever, so plausible that nobody notices the sting. In one sense, this is a victory for the prankster as a tribute to their skill. Alternatively, awful thought, were they so boring that readers lost interest and gave up halfway through?

We will never know in most cases, but Mark Cocker still ruefully recalls how one of the densest newspaper April Fool's ever constructed – densest in terms of jokes per line – failed to go off. Cocker is one of the country's leading experts on birds and he also writes regularly for the *Guardian*'s Country Diary. In 1991 he realised that his slot was going to fall, for the first time, on April the first. 'I decided to see if anyone was awake,' he says. Into 334 lines he crammed 18 spoofs and sent the contribution off. It sailed past the sub-editors, who knew little about nature, but it sailed past the readers as well. Here it is, for you to pit your scientific wits against (although you need to be pretty hot on Britain's flora, fauna, landscape and climate to identify all Mark's pranks).

WEYLAND WOOD, Norfolk: This National Trust reserve is one of the last fragments of ancient woodland in the county and is rich in historical associations. It was mentioned in William II's Domesday Book, although its name, derived from the Celtic word, 'Wanelund', meaning 'place of Wane' (a pagan deity of the Britons), suggests that it was a site of worship in pre-Christian times. One can still find medieval boundaries beneath the trees, while a medieval folk-tale associated with Weyland is supposed to have been the inspiration for Babes in the Wood, the eighteenth-century novel of Norfolk-born author Charles Kingsley. Today the area is better known for its rich community of birds and flowers. Most striking of all is the golden pheasant, with its crimson hood and brilliant yellow underparts. The species is originally from India and was introduced into Britain in the eighteenth century by the Duke of Norfolk. Since then a feral population has established itself in the Broads and a few other county sites. At dawn the males loudly advertise their presence with a jay-like crowing, although seeing one of the world's most colourful creatures is never simple, since they are intensely shy. Equally impossible to pin down are Weyland's hyperactive willow and marsh tits. These identical twins are two of the most difficult of Britain's common birds to separate. In fact it was not until 1895, when the Swiss naturalist Ernst Hartert made a famous discovery on Hampstead Heath, that the marsh tit was recognised as a common species in this country. Fortunately, the woodland flowers are far easier to locate. In late spring there are spectacular stands of bluebells, while early purple orchid and yellow archangel are both common. The intention of our visit, however, was to find a Norfolk rarity and Weyland's speciality yellow star-of-Bethlehem. When we chanced upon a flowering bulb with linear leaves and six yellow petals it seemed we had succeeded. However the literature revealed that this species does not flower until July and that we had obviously made a mistake. The question is, how many?

A nice little pay-off line; but, alas, no one was awake, or else they were too trusting of Mark's authority as a nature writer. Just one thoughtful woman reader wrote in to suggest, with deferential caution, that he might have been over-hasty to dismiss his initial identification of the yellow Star of Bethlehem as a mistake. Her flora suggested that it did indeed flower in spring and not July. 'One down, 17 to go,' says Mark, who is still forlornly waiting for his joke to go off. Even the Star of Bethlehem evaded complete exposure. It isn't found in the part of Norfolk he was describing.

If you can find the answers to Mark's misbehaviour, add them to your collection of the secret April Fool's in this book. But he wasn't the only one. Another *Guardian* colleague, Oliver Burkeman, disappeared up his own formidable powers of parody when he interviewed a non-existent celebrity called Harmony Cousins as the paper's April Fool in 2002 using the style of almost all magazines including the *Guardian's* own G2 section. Yet another vacuous starlet arriving late, yet another 15-minute interview under a publicist's thumb, yet another piece padded out with the writer's descriptions of the hotel, the food, his own feelings and his family life to fill the gap left by his subject's lack of interest and opinions. It was so close to the real thing that it passed almost unnoticed. Readers must have been so lulled by the familiar that they failed to spot clues such as the claim that 'it was the 17th century philosopher Leibniz, of course, who said that "fame is a funny old thing"'.

Oliver recalls ruefully today that he originally put in much more in the same vein, but it was removed to make the spoof subtler. His regrets were heightened by the fact that the *Guardian* was one of only two British newspapers which ran April Fool's that year. The *Sun* rediscovered a dodo (in Bournemouth) and also carried an advertisement which was to become famous, for Tesco's whistling carrots. Everyone else held back because the Queen Mother had died the day before at the age of 101 and their pages were filled with expressions of sorrow and tributes. Everyone except that old royal-basher Mohamed Fayed, that is, whose floating Harrod's prank is described on page 128.

Cleverness is one thing; crudity another. April Fool's jokes have crashed, and in the process also earned the whole genre a bad reputation, by being too cruel or unkind. An example is the case of Glenn Howlett who worked for the city council in the Canadian city of London, a place otherwise famous as the birthplace of the co-discoverer of insulin, Dr Frederick Banting, and the home of Karen Baldwin, who was Miss Universe in 1982. Howlett worked his way up the city hall ladder for 30 years and in November 2003 he was manager of community services and responsible for preparing a major strategy report. He had taken some holiday to think about this, when a memo arrived at his home from the newly appointed city clerk Kevin Bain, saying that the document was due early – by, guess when, April the first.

Howlett cancelled his remaining holiday plans, phoned subordinates to speed into action, suffered heart palpitations and then collapsed with severe stress. Invalided off work, he decided that trying to meet the deadline would be too risky for his health and began negotiations for early retirement. Only then did aghast colleagues, who included the city manager, the acting head of finance and the city engineer, pluck up the courage to confess to their April Fool.

It all turned into the biggest sensation since pioneers arrived at the place in 1796 and caused international controversy by naming somewhere so obscure after the British capital (they also called the local river the Thames and an adjoining patch of forest Westminster). The governor of Canada protested that this was unacceptable for somewhere he 'could only reach by hot air balloon', but London it stayed. The British government was too busy with the aftermath of the American rebellion to risk upsetting even more colonials.

Back in the 20th century, Howlett threatened to sue, a multi-thousand dollar compensation deal was done and the mayor, Anne Marie DeCiccio, admitted 'it's not our finest hour'. Claims and counterclaims swirled round, suggesting that pranks were a council tradition and Howlett had previously taken part in them, but then everyone clammed up. London's 3,000 civic employees were forbidden to play April Fool's in office time ever again. A final statement from the council tried to put the lid on it all: 'While the city appreciates the need for camaraderie within the work environment, any conduct involving practical jokes does not conform to the city's code of ethics.'

The debacle wasn't the worst in the history of crass April Fool's. The *Opinia* newspaper in Romania probably takes that title with its claim in 2000 that sixty long-term prisoners were to be released from the notorious Baia Mare jail. It may have been a piece of political wishful thinking, but it didn't play well with relatives who made the long journey to the prison on April the first to discover that the announcement was a hoax. But repercussions of the Howlett affair still rumble on. In a plea for perspective, Professor Heinz Klatt of the local King's University College told the *London Free Press* that his colleagues were starting to shy away from joking with students. 'People have done pranks all through history,' he said. 'We can live without them, but they add a little light-heartedness. We should keep space for this.'

Part of the deal, though, is assessing the likely reaction of the victim, which the funsters in London, Ontario, got so horribly wrong. A few months ago I was listening on the car radio to a lively phone-in on Radio Five Live about divorce when a listener called Ranjit from Birmingham phoned in. Amid all the bitter anecdotes he struck an oddly jaunty note as he described how he had served papers on his wife as she had morning tea in bed. This came two weeks after a light-hearted chat they'd had in which he'd asked her: 'Would you ever divorce me?' and she'd replied: 'Of course, like a shot.' It wasn't a very good line and the presenter Victoria Derbyshire struggled to keep pace – as I did – while Ranjit described how he'd gone straight off to a lawyer, got the papers drawn up and offered his wife a few minutes to sign them while he had breakfast with some mates down-stairs. When he popped back up, she was in floods of tears. Appalling or what? But then there was a big brummy giggle and Ranjit said: 'Of course you know what the date was, don't you Victoria?' More bafflement. 'It was April the first, of course.' And the lawyer who did the papers was called April and something which sounded very much like Fool. 'Well Ranjit,' said Victoria, 'are you still together? Because you're a lucky man if you are.' It turned out that the happy couple were into their 22nd year of marriage. Ranjit's wife is clearly a resilient and basically foolproof person and for that sort of victim, anything goes.

One entire category which is seldom capable of taking such a relaxed and forgiving attitude is the range of authorities which have to handle the fallout of mass fools. They form a separate category of secondary victims, but often get much more fed up with April Foolers than the people who have actually been deceived. Not surprisingly. Take South Kesteven council in Lincolnshire, which in 1992 had to field a blizzard of phone calls about its plans to spend £150,000 on a statue of Margaret Thatcher, celebrated daughter of a Grantham grocer. There were no such plans except in the imaginations of the April Fool team at the local *Grantham Trader*, but the public's fury at the proposed 'waste of public money' was borne out by the cost of council staff time, stationery and phone bills in trying to nail the stunt before it went national.

Causing chaos for public authorities is a freequent effect of American April Foolers, partly because of the large number of natural and man-made disasters with which their vast country is always threatened. In 1999 an Oregon radio station triggered a mass evacuation in the city's Ochoco Creek suburb by announcing that the upriver dam had burst. Likewise, DJs in Virginia Beach jammed the local 911 emergency lines in 1992 when they reported that a build-up of methane gas was about to explode at the local rubbish tip (wittily nicknamed Mount Trashmore). Severe reprimands followed in both cases and radio station staff were suspended without pay.

The blame can also lie partly with victims in these cases. Arizonans who panicked about Operation Killer Bee in 1994 should have paid more attention to the text of leaflets posted in their mailboxes. These instructed residents to stay indoors from 9.30 a.m. to 2.30 p.m. on April the first because of dangerously poisonous aerial spraying to wipe out the insects. A lot of calls to the police and public health services would have been saved if readers had sussed the initial letters of the suspiciously cumbersome Arizona Pest Removal Information Line (For Outside Operations Listings).

Irritation and potentially disastrous results have increased with the internationalisation of April Fool's, through ever-expanding mass communications. Horace de Vere Cole's pioneering wheeze of invading France at the head of a German army detachment, fortunately stopped by his university friends, has an increasing number of imitators. Some misfired because their authors were, well, not really used to the subtlety and light touch which mark successful fooling. Thus the Russian news agency ITAR-TASS caused genuine if brief diplomatic confusion in 1996 when it announced that the parliament in Moscow was considering a revival of the Warsaw Pact. Way further offbeam was the prank by an Israeli army intelligence officer who planted a spoof item in his unit's monitoring service report in 1986 saying that the leader of the Shi'ite Amal movement Nabih Berri had been assassinated. As the Museum of Hoaxes website observes: 'Hey, nothing says funny like stirring up tension in the Middle East.' The officer was court-martialled but should also have been given some form of re-education in humour for committing gross disservices to April Fooling.

He was working in an area of the world which is not only super-sensitive politically, but also has an interestingly ambivalent attitude

to the day of pranks. Hindus' letting off steam during Holi has no
direct comparison in Islam, and some of the many strands of this
diverse religion do not approve of it at all. The fact that the last
Muslim stronghold in Spain, Granada, fell to the armies of Ferdinand
and Isabella on 1 April 1492 and this was celebrated by the victors as
the 'April trick' is enough for some. Extremists among the extremists
add that 1492 was doubly disastrous as the year that Europe discovered
America. In 2001 the Grand Mufti of Saudi Arabia issued a warning
to Muslims not to take part in April Fool's because they were 'a
practice of the unbelievers'. The statement was issued on 31 March but
it was not an April Fool itself. Within a year it was followed by an
ordinance from the kingdom's Commission for the Promotion of
Virtue and the Prevention of Evil which banned the sale of red roses,
teddy bears and cards associated with St Valentine's Day.

Unlike 14 February, which is associated with a saint, however
loosely these days, April Fool's is not a Christian festival and no one
made any mention of Granada. The Mufti was more concerned with
the deceit which lies at the day's heart. He said: 'It is prohibited because
lying is prohibited at all times and under all conditions.' The only get-
outs were telling untruths in time of war, to bring reconciliation
between people or to protect the honour of a husband or wife.

It may have been the first of these which encouraged the amount
of April foolery associated with the Iraqi regime of Saddam Hussein,
although his dictatorship also discouraged theocracy and tended
towards the secular. At all events, the newspaper *Babil* which was
owned by Saddam's son Uday started its own little pranks subculture
in April 1998. Its fake news item that President Clinton had decided
to lift sanctions against Iraq doesn't seem wildly funny or original,
but Uday was satisfied and had another go the following year. This
was slightly more sophisticated in announcing that monthly food
rations were in future going to contain Pepsi-Cola, bananas and
chocolate – all associated with the national enemy. That was it so far
as creativity was concerned. In 2000, *Babil* went back to the sanction-
lifting hoax and in 2001 it repeated the banana, Pepsi and chocolate
one. Oh dear.

But that wasn't quite the end of this routine. In April 2003 Iraq was actually at war, a terrible time for April fooling although in the terms of the Saudi Arabian Grand Mufti's statement, at least a state of affairs where lying could be permissible. On April the first, Saddam Hussein's ambassador in Moscow, Abbas Khalaf Kunfuth, called a press conference and announced to shocked journalists that an American nuclear missile had been fired accidentally at British units during the advance on Basra and towns south of Baghdad. There was a silence and then Kunfuth delightedly beamed: 'April Fool.' Eight days later US troops occupied the centre of the Iraqi capital and Saddam's regime (and along with it Kunfuth's job) was declared officially to be at an end.

Given these moments of practical joking, it is appropriate that one of the men behind the rapid collapse of Saddam Hussein's defences was an agent codenamed April Fool. According to General Tommy Franks, who commanded the 2003 invasion, this man was an American army officer befriended by an Iraqi diplomat in New York who was really an agent of the regime. The CIA and FBI were already on to the Iraqi but decided, in the best crafty tradition of turning hostile agents, to use the US army officer to feed the spy misleading material. The nickname April Fool may have been a nod in the direction of Uday's dismal pranks, but the deceit worked. The Iraqi went home gleefully with what he thought was the coalition plan for an invasion from the north, where Saddam Hussein then uselessly stationed some of his crack troops. Subsequent events in the long and bloody years of the Iraq occupation, it has to be added, may raise the question in some minds: who are the fools now?

WHOOPS, SILLY ME

DEPUTY DAWG

The sheriff's office in Florida's Broward county is usually a pretty run-of-the-mill law enforcement joint, but that changed with case number PB04-04-00333 on 1 April 2004. Following the usual laconic style, the crime report lists the suspect as Paul Michael Goobie, 47, male, and the victims as Kevin Meloy, 42, male, and a chihuahua dog. What happened was this. Prankster Goobie had been to see the film *National Lampoon's Vacation* in which Chevy Chase ties a dog to the bumper of his car and then forgetfully drives off. When he found a dead chihuahua in the street on his way to work with ABC Cutting Contractors in North Lauderdale, he remembered the date and couldn't resist a prank. So it was that his co-worker Meloy headed for home to Pompano Beach unaware that a dead dog was bouncing along behind his pick-up – or that horrified witnesses were jamming the lines to the sheriff. He was even more unaware because he is deaf, so hooting and shouts went unheard for two miles. As well as tasteless, the April Fool was costly for Goobie. The reason that the dog was listed by the sheriff as a victim in spite of being dead was this: unlawful disposal of a dead animal is a second-degree misdemeanour in the US, punishable by 60 days' jail or a fine of up to $500.

THE FOOLERS FOOLED

Woman's Hour on Radio 4 had a positive festival of foolishness on 1 April 1992, culminating in a deadpan reading from a newly discovered fragment of Jane Austen. It appeared to show the witty but always subtle observer of humanity in a raunchier light. Part of the text read: 'It is a truth universally acknowledged that a single woman in possession of her virginity must be in a state of urgency to lose it.' Dring dring, the office phone jumped after the broadcast with a call from Michael Green, the director of Radio 4. The programme's joint editors Clare Selerie and Sally Feldman and its presenter Jenni Murray were summoned into the presence and given a furious bollocking by Green. Didn't they know even the basic BBC rules? Ums, errs and a tentative 'But didn't you get the memo about our plan?' And then a big grin from Green and a triumphant cry of April Fools. The biters bit.

ROPE TRICK

They say that revenge is a dish best taken cold, but Randy Wood did a little too much planning for an April Fool in 2004 on his ex-wife. The 33-year-old went to elaborate lengths to fake suicide by hanging, using a power line maintenance worker's harness to take his weight while he dangled from a tree in his garden. Then he rang the former Mrs Wood and asked her to come over to his house in West Monroe near Syracuse in upstate New York. She did and naturally flipped, phoning the emergency services who turned out in force. Mr Wood found himself facing a year's jail or a fine of up to $1,000. 'He claims he did it as an April Fool's joke,' said Sherif Reuel Todd of Oswego county. 'But obviously it's not a funny matter.'

SERIOUS FOOLING OFFICE

You can't ask for a higher class of April Fooler than a member of the British police's Serious Fraud Office, but their best-known sally into the field of fun went badly wrong. An officer involved in a complex case decided in 1991 to tease a lawyer colleague by sending him a fax saying that the then Liberal Party leader Sir David Steel was planning to attend a bail hearing and oppose the SFO line on an arrested suspect. The fax included a forged letter from Sir David on House of Commons writing paper and needless to say it got out. The MP was furious. The SFO prankster's lack of judgement was balanced by his skill at forgery and SFO's high command showed expertise at stringing things out. In June 1993 Steel was still complaining that the case had still not been sorted out.

THE FOILER FOILED

It sounds a great idea, but Phillip Chavira chose the wrong colleague for a highly original April Fool's stunt after she did the comparatively boring trick of sealing up his room door with toilet paper. Chavira and two other students in Tucson, Arizona, waited until the young woman had gone out and then covered the entire contents of her room, from TV to work books and pencils, with 400 square feet of cooking foil. It must have looked like a modern artwork with the foil sheet neatly moulded to everything, but the victim felt upset that anyone had invaded her privacy and touched her things. Police were called, the college didn't get the joke and Chavira lost his job as a resident assistant.

A BRIDGE TOO FAR

Four Oxford University students mounted a spectacular April Fool from the soaring Clifton suspension bridge in Bristol in 1979, but had to pay for their daring with hours in court. Long before bungee jumping became commonplace, they attached 150 ft elasticated ropes to Isambard Kingdom Brunel's graceful span and tumbled down into the Avon gorge. They all bounced safely up and down, suffering only a few bruises and rope burns, but the police and magistrates were not amused. The bridge has a reputation for suicides which nobody wants to encourage, and the leap took place in front of a mass of carefully invited reporters and photographers. The bench wasn't taken, either, with the group's organisation, the Oxford University Dangerous Sports Club, or its tie motif of a man in a wheelchair. The father of Tim Hunt, brother of the racing driver James and one of the stunters, said stoutly: 'I'm very glad there are still people around who have the guts to do this sort of thing.' Newspapers saw a spate of letters to the editor demanding suspended sentences and long stretches but the lads were bound over for two years in the sum of £100 each after admitting a breach of the peace.

NO TRUTH IN THE UNTRUTH

Perhaps a bit giddy in the wake of Soviet repression, Russia produced a bumper crop of April Fool's in 1992, among them a story about gay activists planning to cross the Atlantic in huge inflated condoms. The paper *Moskovskaya Pravda* (Moscow Truth) produced an entire special issue dated 32 March and called Moscow Untruth. The dud in the collection was a TV announcement that the disputed South Kurile Islands were to be ceded to Japan after a dispute going back to the Second World War. The islands were paralysed by strikes and protests and the local council chairman Nikolia Pokidin told the ITAR-TASS agency: 'There are limits for any joke. Rubbing salt into this wound is worse than cruel, when for nearly two years of real negotiations the nerves and patience of these islanders have been continually worn away.'

TALL TALES FROM ARABY

Religious worries about lying have not eliminated the April Fool from the Middle East but the genre has a bit of a record for backfiring. In 2001 Kuwaitis protested in large numbers about a government plan to move the iconic concrete Kuwaiti Towers from opposite the Emir's palace to a tribal area, allegedly as part of a rural development plan. Other Kuwaitis were miffed when they turned up with picnics to watch the spectacular operation – exclusively revealed by a local newspaper – and nothing happened. It was hardly to be expected: the tallest of the three concrete spires topped with huge spheres measures 613 ft (187 m). But then Kuwait has enough oil money to do practically anything. A Syrian newspaper, *Tishrin*, meanwhile announced startlingly generous $60 monthly payments for the unemployed to be paid for out of the recovery of $50 billion stolen from the national treasury and spirited to overseas bank accounts. The risky satire also made headlines in neighbouring Jordan where the official news agency Petra swallowed it and later had to issue an apology. Four science students hoaxed by an April Fooler in Lebanon were meanwhile so cross that they invented a counter-stunt about the Syrians staging a kidnap on campus. Beirut university was temporarily closed, the Lebanese defence minister took charge of an inquiry and the pranksters were arrested.

THE PHANTOM WEDDING

I don't know what to make of this one, but maybe you will. In 1979 Mike Webster and Sally Young were due to get married in the London suburb of Southfields. It turned out to be a peculiar do. Mike and a friend called Eamonn Walsh, both 24 and both computer operators, spent three months organising an engagement party, wedding invitations, a stag party and finally pre-ceremony drinks on 1 April, when their weird prank was revealed. Friends had asked occasionally why Sally never seemed to be around and now they discovered. She didn't exist. Mike and Eamonn had made the whole thing up, including a complete personality for the fake bride. She was a brown-eyed student from Brunel University, with long auburn hair, a 34-25-36 figure and parents who insisted she went home to see them in the country every weekend. It's a surprise that Mike wasn't bopped by his pals, who had bought him and Sally a present with a whip round and put on their best suits and buttonholes for the day. But they didn't, and he told the following day's *Sun*: 'I've no plans for the real thing. I haven't even got a girlfriend at the moment.' Surprise.

MANY DEAD

The ultimate in victim-packed April Fool's was a film by Fred Walton which premiered in 1986 and starred nobody famous. This was just as well because like a 17th-century revenger's tragedy, nearly everyone ended up dead. The movie was called *April Fool's Day* and the action was set entirely on April the first, with an American teen called Muffy St John inviting becoming pals to her parents' secluded luxury island home for the time of their lives. Or as the publicity put it, 'the last time of their lives'. All the ingenious bloodbaths of the horror genre were employed, with much tongue-in-cheekery. Sample dialogue: 'Relax honey.' 'Three people are dead and you're telling me to relax?' Throat-cutting, decapitation, hanging, castration, it's all here and for once Michael Leapman's doom-mongering rings true: 'If there was nothing in last week's crop of spoofs as traumatic as the loss of a daughter,' he complained, referring all the way back to Ceres and Proserpina, 'most added a gratuitous element of irritation and inconvenience to the lives of people who already endure enough of both.'

Envoi

All good things must come to an end.

ENGLISH PROVERB/STAR TREK: THE NEXT GENERATION

*t*HIS BOOK HAS TOLD THE STORY OF AN ANCIENT TRADITION BUT ONE WHICH OVER THE CENTURIES HAS MOVED IN ALTERNATING LEAPS AND LIMPS. There have been years in which the world's appetite for April Foolery has seemed insatiable – the Romans, the medieval monks, the Barnumite Americans. And there have also been times when farting cushions and itching powder were suppressed or unknown. Like so many social customs, the one has tended to follow the other. The wheel has turned. And so it is no surprise that we are now moving from three decades of pranking overdrive into a period of calm.

I can tell you this with certainty because a friend of mine has an in to the Media Liaison Group which meets at the end of every tax year to discuss informal ways of limiting unnecessary competition at a time of intense and potentially disastrous rivalry. No one wants an actual cartel but since the breakthrough of new technology the various companies have found it useful to avoid wasting money and talent by quietly dropping expensive extras in a discreet mutual truce.

Thus imitation leather binders for your papers, which once vied in the softness of their covers and the richness of their gold tooling, are a thing of the past. Kiddies' clubs with their dubious prizes involving junk food and the clear threat of paedophile interest and sky-high lawsuits have also faded away. And last year, after a succession of false starts, it was at last the turn of April Fool's. Look guys, said the preliminary circular to MLG delegates two months before the meeting, is this another area where we could all agree to take things easy for a while?

The actual editors of our great newspapers are much too busy, and perhaps a bit grand, to spend time on this sort of thing. So it was their managing editors, a hapless collection of ex-journalists doing a job which no one else wants to do, who got together to hammer an agreement out. In a coyly self-referential move, they met at Fleet Street's famous Cheshire Cheese pub on April 1st last year and devoted a couple of drink-enhanced hours to debate.

The starting point for the discussion was a leader in *The Times* as long ago as 1993 which suggested that mass joking of the type which had followed San Serriffe was driving out genuine fun. 'The time may have come to call a halt,' it said, and *The Times* bravely went ahead alone and did just that. The only April Fool in the paper was an advertisement from that larky chap the Comptroller General of the Patent Office. Several other paid-for ad spoofs had actually been turned down and *The Times* embarked on a self-denying approach from that year on.

Addressing the MLG meeting, the *Times* rep Ian Moltear admitted that this had been a solo effort for the best part of a decade; but it was now clear that uneasiness had spread. Nora Mighpal from the *Telegraph* website agreed with a passion. She quoted from a recent discussion on the online forum of Anime News, a website which has a long tradition of ambushing its users with an April Fool. For the first time last year, they didn't. Nora read to the meeting the 7.08 a.m. post from the Anime team in Indianapolis in response to users' questions: why no prank?

'There aren't going to be any April Fool's shenanigans this year. We of the staff had a discussion about it and a majority agreed that ANN's reputation made it improper for us to do something of that nature, given how easily postings on a well-known site like ours could be misconstrued as truth. (No matter how ridiculous it might sound, you know someone would believe it and start spreading it around.) Sorry to disappoint, guys.' At 9.33 a.m. the editor-in-chief chipped in with an additional note: 'Problem is, the best April Fool's jokes are the ones people believe. However, ANN absolutely can't be in the position where it is propagating falsehoods. Not any more at least. So the only option left are unbelievable April Fool's jokes. Things that are funny, but not convincing.'

And that was it. Did the punters rebel? No, they were weary of it all too. One called Zac seemed to speak for them when he posted at 11.38 a.m.: 'Personally, I think the whole "fake news on april fool's day!" thing is so overdone as to not really be all that funny anymore. Every site on the internet does it and it's not so gut-bustingly hilarious that it's worth the 400 emails over the next 3 months from people asking me if those stories were true or not . . . to stick to something simply because of tradition and not because we actually have something really hilarious to post is kinda backwards, IMO.'

IMO – internet shorthand for 'in my opinion'. And it was the opinion of everyone at the Cheshire Cheese, as dusk started to fall and deadlines neared back at the office, that an idea shared by outlets as different as *The Times* and Anime News Network could only be right. Teri Mehen of *The Irish Times* moved the resolution agreeing an experimental one-year breathing space; there were plenty of seconders and a unanimous Yes vote. And that is why – however weird and unlikely some of the stories seem (see Chapter 9) – there will be no April Fool's in the British media this year for the first time. The truce is experimental and how long it will last is unknown. Let's leave that to the prophets.

SELECT BIBLIOGRAPHY

de Jaeger, Charles. *The Linz File: Hitler's Plunder of Europe's Art*. Webb & Bower 1981. Another side of the spaghetti man.

Dimbleby, Jonathan. *Richard Dimbleby: A Biography*. Hodder & Stoughton 1975. Explains why so many believed in the spag.

Fitzsimons, Raymund. *Barnum in London*. Geoffrey Bles 1969. Good stuff on the ultimate showman.

Lindley, Richard. *Panorama: Fifty Years of Pride and Paranoia*. Politico's 2002. Not much spaghetti but lots else.

MacDougall, Curtis D. *Hoaxes*. Dover Publications 1940, 1958. Invaluable.

Pope, T. Michael (ed.). *The Book of Fleet Street*. Cassell 1930. Pranks in London.

Stephen, Adrian. *The Dreadnought Hoax*. The Hogarth Press 1936. Told by Virginia Woolf's brother and fellow member of the spoofing gang.

Taylor, Geoffrey. *Changing Faces: A History of the Guardian 1956–88*. Fourth Estate 1983. Modestly says too little about San Serriffe.

Waterhouse, Robert. *The Other Fleet Street*. First Edition 2004. Japes in Manchester.

Weber, R.L., and R. Mendoza. *A Random Walk in Science*. Institute of Physics 1973. Physicists can be really fun.

The Museum of Hoaxes: www.museumofhoaxes.com. Much the best of innumerable April Fool-related websites.

Wikipedia: www.wikipedia.org. The second-best, and gaining.

INDEX